YOUR
PENSION

YOUR PENSION

The Complete Guide to Pension Planning in Canada

Patrick Longhurst, FCIA
and Rose Marie Earle, MBA

Doubleday Canada Limited

Typesetting by Compeer Typographic Services Limited
Printed in Canada by Gagne Printing

Design: Ross Mah Design Associates
Illustration: Terry Dovastan

Canadian Cataloguing in Publication Data

Longhurst, Patrick
    Your pension

Rev. ed.
First ed. (1987) published under title: Looking after
the future.
Includes bibliographical references.
IBSN 0-385-25269-2

1. Pensions – Canada.   2. Old age pensions – Canada.
I. Earle, Rose Marie, 1946-   . II. Title.
III. Title: Looking after the future.

HD7129.L66 1990   331.25′2′0971   C90-093702-5

Published in Canada by
Doubleday Canada Limited
105 Bond Street
Toronto, Ontario
M5B 1Y3

Contents

Introduction

Knowledge is power.
Francis Bacon

"WILL YOU STILL NEED ME? Will you still feed me? When I'm sixty-four?" It seems unlikely that Paul, George, and Ringo will have to worry about where their next meals are coming from when they retire. However, those lyrics could be the theme for most Canadians who apparently are blithely assuming that someone else will look after them when they retire.

In the first edition of this book we reported on a 1985 study prepared for the Department of Health and Welfare in Ottawa. The report concluded that "the average Canadian is either not consciously planning for his or her retirement income security, or if they are, they are building on a foundation of ignorance." The news in 1990 was not much better! A Gallup Canada Inc. survey report in an August 1990 *Globe and Mail* said more than one-third of Canadians have no savings or investment programs for retirement. The 1990 report concluded that many Canadians are ill-prepared for retirement and some will simply not be able to retire! The aim of this book is to overcome some of the ignorance concerning pension plans and to help Canadians make realistic preparations for retirement.

Most of us are looking forward to retirement. We dream about the things we'll be able to do with all that extra time. We'll travel, devote more time to a hobby or try a new career. Statistics tell us that Canadians are retiring earlier and living longer. This means that most of us will be retired for a relatively long time. Will retirement be as pleasant as we think it will be? Will we have the financial resources to do the things we want to do?

We've watched friends of our parents, the parents of our friends, or perhaps even our parents retire. The reality has not always been as pleasant as we thought it would be. Savings swallowed up by inflation, little or no company pension, and modest government benefits have left many retired people inadequately prepared financially to fulfil all of their expectations.

There are many things to consider when thinking about retirement — your health, what you will do with your leisure time, how your spouse will adjust, for example — but financial security is probably the most important consideration.

Ensuring financial security in retirement is the purpose of pensions, whether they are provided by the government (public), employers (private), or our own personal savings (RRSPs, stocks, and bonds, for example). The aim of this book is to help you assess your financial planning for retirement. It will enable you to determine what your resources will be and whether those resources will be adequate to meet your retirement needs. It will give you the knowledge to select those options available in the pension system that are right for you.

Part I provides a brief introduction to the various sources of retirement income. Part II introduces you to some typical Canadians and describes what you can expect from government plans. Part III outlines some of the important aspects of private pension plans and Part IV will help you decide how your personal plans can work in concert with government and employer plans to provide the level of income you will need in retirement.

Unlike some who have written about the Canadian pension system, we have no axe to grind. There are some shortcomings in the current pension system. However, we believe that if you know and understand what you have to work with, you will be in a better position to achieve your personal retirement dreams.

Basic changes in Canadian society have fuelled the need for better retirement planning. Lifestyles are changing so rapidly and so radically that it is now necessary for each person or couple to prepare in advance for a well-financed retirement. Gone are the days when you could count on being looked after by your children or other relatives. The nuclear family and high divorce rates mean that many Canadians have only themselves to count on when they retire. Retired Canadians are living longer and high inflation has made their pensions inadequate in their later years. Increased job mobility means that many Canadians have little or no pension from private companies. The aging of the "baby boomers" means that many of the issues can no longer be ignored.

These factors led to almost a decade of debate about the Canadian pension system. The federal government and virtually every provincial government studied pensions and came up with solutions to some of the problems. Part III refers to the provincial consensus. This is a loose term to describe the results of their studies.

Because of the autonomy of each province, uniform pension legislation across Canada has been a voluntary process. Starting with a public conference in Quebec City, in 1975, CAPSA (the Canadian Association of Pension Supervisory Authorities) attempted to ensure that each province and the federal government would take a common approach to the major pension issues. In reality this was an unobtainable goal. After all, each province has a different political orientation and each region of the country has different priorities and different economic situations.

The consensus referred to is the common position taken by Ontario and the federal government. This position is close to that taken by Quebec and Alberta although somewhat removed from the existing legislation in Manitoba and Saskatchewan.

The exceptions to the consensus are not listed on every occasion. Instead, Appendix I provides detailed recommendations by province for those readers who are interested.

Although uniformity of pension legislation wasn't achieved completely, many changes have been announced which affect government pensions, private pensions, and personal savings plans — changes that will help Canadians plan better for their retirement years. We will discuss these changes throughout the book as we deal with each layer of the Canadian pension system.

Acknowledgements

Many people helped make this book a reality. We appreciate the support provided by our employer, Johnson & Higgins Willis Faber Ltd. We are especially grateful to Joe Knope, who believed we could do it; Angie Felgendreher, who gave us her help and enthusiasm; Brenda Babineau, who patiently typed endless drafts; and Dean Apps and Susan Smith, who reviewed the manuscript and offered valuable suggestions.

For their early encouragement we thank Susan Deller, Robin Schiele, and Andrea and Barry Vincent. We are also indebted to the Honourable Douglas Frith, MP; the Honourable Jake Epp, Minister of Health and Welfare; the Honourable Paul Hellyer; and Robert White, President, Canadian Auto Workers, for their helpful comments which gave us new insight into the subject.

Finally, our spouses, Laura Longhurst and David Hynes, endured through the many months of our work and we owe them a very special thanks.

PART I

OVERVIEW

1

From Here To Annuity

*pension/Pen-chən/n: a fixed sum paid regularly
esp. to a person retired from service.*
The Merriam-Webster Dictionary

BEFORE WE GO TOO FAR, we must understand just what pension
plans are and how they evolved into the pension system we have in
Canada today. Basically, a pension is a sum of money paid, usually
monthly, to a retired person. In this chapter we describe the development of the Canadian pension system and give you an overview
of government and private pension plans.

Modern pension plans owe their birth to the dislocation of society
caused by the Industrial Revolution. In the late nineteenth century,
as the western world shifted from an agricultural to an industrial
economy, society took a hard look at older people and decided that
industrialization was for the young. Before the Industrial Revolution, people did not retire. Most couldn't afford to stop working
and only did so when they were physically unable to continue. As
this was the period when the extended family was common, the
elderly usually lived with their families and children and were
respected and revered for their wisdom and experience.

Industrialization changed all of that. Workers migrated to the
cities and the extended family began to break up. Sons and daugh-
ters were seldom able to take care of older parents. The Industrial
Revolution also had an effect on the status of the older worker.
While industry might like us to believe that it began to establish
retirement programs to reward long and faithful service, self-interest

probably had a lot more to do with it. Mandatory retirement for older workers served to create a more efficient workforce, to facilitate the transfer of skills from one generation to another, and to help stabilize the existing social order. Many older workers lost their jobs because it was widely believed that younger people were better able to operate high-speed machinery and were more productive. Manufacturing companies adopted restrictive hiring practices with regard to older people and established mandatory retirement programs. They believed the words of a 1945 study entitled *Employee Retirement Plans* that "at some point in an employee's working life the value acquired with increasing length of service . . . will no longer offset the effects of the aging process." As the Industrial Revolution moved ahead, retirement programs began to appear in the transportation industry, particularly in railway companies. The railways, it seems, were liable for damages resulting from train accidents and one way of reducing that liability, they thought, was to remove older, supposedly accident-prone workers.

Along with the breakdown of the extended family, industrialization brought with it another important force that helped the spread of pension plans — the trade union movement. Initially, trade unions sponsored some of their own pension plans. Then, in 1948, pensions were recognized by the U.S. Supreme Court as a legitimate bargaining point in contract negotiations and the stage was set for their spread throughout North America. But even unions were not totally altruistic in seeking pension plans for their members. Trade unions saw retirement as a way of easing in a new generation of workers and limiting numbers in industries where there were too many workers.

As industrialization continued to contribute to the breakdown in the extended family, many people came to believe that society had a responsibility to care for its weaker members. People began to look to their employers, their unions, and especially their government to protect them against want in old age.

The idea of government pension schemes originated in Western Europe and Britain. The first national old-age insurance system was established by Otto von Bismarck, Chancellor of Germany, in the 1880s. It is Bismarck who is generally credited with establishing a fixed age for retirement, initially age sixty-five. Canada was far behind. It was 1927 when the federal government first intervened directly in the slowly expanding pension system. Now we have two government-sponsored plans plus a supplementary means-tested plan.

The Canadian pension system can be compared to a three-legged stool. Government-sponsored plans are one leg, employer- or association-sponsored (private) plans form the second leg, and personal savings plans represent the third leg. Personal savings can mean just about any personal financial arrangement — from burning the mortgage on your home to risking everything in the stock market — as long as the long-term goal is a nest-egg for your retirement. More and more, for the average Canadian, this personal plan means enjoying the tax advantages of a Registered Retirement Savings Plan (RRSP). Despite a slow start when they were introduced almost thirty years ago, RRSPs have become a significant part of pension planning as Canadians begin to realize that private and government plans alone can't provide the level of income they want (or need) in retirement.

Government Plans—The 25 Percent Solution

Government-sponsored pension plans will provide the foundation for your retirement income. In discussions of the Canadian pension system the suggestion is frequently made that government pension schemes should be expanded. Indeed, the government's role in providing Canadians with retirement income has undergone vast changes since our representatives in the House of Commons first began discussing the care of the aged in 1906.

The concern in 1906 was no doubt influenced by developments in other countries. Germany had introduced a contributory plan (workers shared the cost) for all wage earners and lower-paid salaried employees in the 1880s. Denmark and New Zealand had means-tested plans (if you had the means you failed the test). While Canada continued to discuss the issue, a Commonwealth of Australia plan was introduced, and a limited plan was established in the United Kingdom (it was to exclude "wastrels and loafers").

Following the lead of these more aggressive societies, Canada saw the need for a government pension system. The main hurdle to its establishment was the same one that complicates so many issues in Canada: would it come under federal or provincial jurisdiction?

Prevailing judicial interpretation of the British North America Act held that any form of social reform came under provincial jurisdiction. However, a clever invention — the "grant-in-aid" — finally got the government into pensions in 1927. The Old Age Pensions Act offered federal grants-in-aid to provinces that passed enabling legislation. The grants were to pay 50 percent (later changed to 75 percent) of the cost of non-contributory means-tested pensions. The maximum pension would be $20 a month to persons over age seventy who met certain citizenship and residence requirements.

The plan finally became national when the last two provinces, Quebec and New Brunswick, joined in 1936 and 1937. The benefit level was increased to $25 in 1943, to $30 in 1947, and to $40 in 1949 as the result of wartime and postwar inflation. But, until 1952, it remained a means-tested plan for the "aged and deserving poor."

The Old Age Pensions Act was replaced with the universal Old Age Security (OAS) Act on January 1, 1952, with the only stipulation being a residence test. The OAS Act paid pensions of $40 a month at age seventy, and introduced means-tested pensions of $40 a month for those aged sixty-five to sixty-nine. Benefits for both pensions were increased several times over the next fifteen years. They reached $46 in July 1957, $55 later that year, $65 in early 1962, and $75 in late 1963. It seems that pensioners were of most concern to the politicians when an election was in the offing!

As time went on, discussion began to centre on the possibility of introducing a national plan to which workers would contribute (the OAS is non-contributory and is financed through general taxation). A report in 1959 studied the issue but failed to make a recommendation. Work on a contributory plan continued within the federal bureaucracy but no legislation was proposed until after the 1963 election. During that election the Liberal party included the Canada Pension Plan as one of the major planks of its platform.

In her book *Memoirs of a Bird in a Gilded Cage* the late Judy LaMarsh devotes considerable space to the controversial development of the Canada Pension Plan (CPP). LaMarsh was the Minister of Health and Welfare in Lester B. Pearson's first cabinet and, as such, was responsible for the development of the CPP and its passage by Parliament.

As part of the election platform LaMarsh said the plan was "one of the most detailed programs ever put before an electorate." There was an election folder about the plan; "most candidates handed it out but hardly anyone made speeches about it because they couldn't understand it." As luck would have it, the new Liberal government adopted "Sixty Days of Decision" as the slogan for its early days in office. The CPP was to be part of the fruits of that first sixty days of activity. With all of the questions to be resolved about what form the plan would take, not to mention negotiations with the provinces to ensure the plan would be universal and portable, it soon became obvious that the legislation couldn't be introduced in the 1963 parliamentary session. Instead the government settled for producing a White Paper to explain the scheme first.

LaMarsh describes briefly, but probably accurately, how the decision to make the plan fully effective in ten years was arrived at. The first choice was to allow workers who had paid even one instalment of contributions and then went on pension to receive full benefits immediately. The second choice was to begin paying full benefits only after twenty years' service, that is, participants would have to work and contribute for at least twenty years before they "earned" a pension. But, as LaMarsh notes, "a scheme which didn't come into effect fully for another twenty years didn't make much sense in solving the social problems of the day (nor was it very sexy politically), so we early resolved to make it a ten-year vesting plan — the constant Canadian compromise at work."

Compromise was also necessary to ensure that Quebec became part of the CPP. The province had worked out its own scheme but, after negotiations, agreed to certain compromises in order that the pension plan would be universal. However, it had to have a separate name. It's the Quebec Pension Plan in Quebec, but in the rest of Canada it's the Canada Pension Plan.

Other problems beset the proposed plan. Life insurance companies were opposed to a universal pension scheme. They were worried about the effect it would have on their business of selling company (private) pension plans. Lobbying by the insurance companies was fierce, especially during an election campaign in Ontario. But they failed to stop the CPP and eventually LaMarsh got her revenge for what she called their "cussedly troublesome" meddling. The Bill was through Parliament and LaMarsh, her officials, and an advertising agency were planning how to present the details of the CPP to the public. The idea was to use photos of people of various ages and walks of life. When they were picking the representative photos and names LaMarsh claims she had the last laugh: "I chose the name for the final gentleman — Clark Kilgore, a play on the names of Mr. Clarke, that pain-in-the-neck pension expert from British Columbia, and David Kilgour" (Kilgour was president of Great-West Life Assurance Company and a major lobbyist against the CPP).

The difficulties in coming up with an advertising campaign provided some of the lighter moments in what was generally a disheartening experience for the novice Cabinet minister. In seeking representative Canadians, the ad agency had developed a tape for radio presentation: "They had chosen as an example a cowboy — a cowboy, of all things! — and the tape was full of the sound of cattle bellowing and cowboys yipping and dogs barking, to introduce the cowboy and describe the pension benefits he might achieve after a lifetime in the saddle. It sounded like a reincarnation of 'Hi-Ho, Silver!' and it stunk!" Equally amusing was her reaction to the first CPP symbol the ad agency suggested: "a kind of Disney squirrel, cuddling a large acorn to its breast. There was no question it got across the idea of saving for the future, but a squirrel. And a squirrel with a nut. I imagined what I would have done with that had I been in Opposition."

Paul Hellyer, who is probably best known for unifying the Canadian armed forces when he was Pearson's Minister of Defence, contends in his autobiography that LaMarsh was really a pawn in the game of introducing the Canada Pension Plan. Hellyer maintains that the "plan was really the child of Walter Gordon and Tom Kent." (Gordon was Finance Minister and Kent was — as Judy LaMarsh described him — "the Prime Minister's chief adviser, an absolutely brilliant idea-man.") LaMarsh maintained that "the Pension Plan would never have come into being at all without [Kent]," and Hellyer seems to agree. "I was never absolutely sure which one [Gordon or Kent] was the father and which the mother but more or less concluded that most of the ideas originated with Kent and were instantly adopted as Walter's own, although it really didn't matter. This plan, like most of their policies, was complicated in the extreme."

Hellyer was strongly critical of the proposed plan within Cabinet. One of his main concerns was the impact on the economy of a pay-as-you-go plan (the income basically balancing the outgo). Hellyer wanted a fully funded plan (in which each individual's pension would be paid for before he or she retired). That way the government would have the funds available for its economic goal of buying back Canada.

Because Hellyer didn't like the proposed plan, the prime minister challenged him to produce a new one and gave him ten days to do it!

Hellyer came up with a plan that was "in effect . . . like a Registered Retirement Savings Plan for each individual Canadian. From the day an individual began their first job their contributions, together with those of their employer, would go into their personalized fund as a tax-deductible investment trust. Self-employed persons would pay both employer and employee shares."

Hellyer envisioned that the individual would be able to choose the financial institution in which to invest his or her money. An amount could be moved from one institution to another at set intervals if the contributor was dissatisfied with the investment return. Finally, the fund would be used to buy a lifetime annuity any time after age sixty.

Hellyer particularly liked his plan because it would mean that existing private plans could be broken up (assets would have been distributed pro rata to the individual accounts). He envisioned that the Old Age Pension plan could be phased out because it would no longer be needed. As Hellyer saw it, his plan would not only provide adequate, fully portable pensions for all working Canadians, but it also would allow "governments to ultimately retire from the pension business with all its temptations and complications and create a massive pool of capital sufficient for Canadians to develop their own mines, mills and smelters." But Hellyer's plan, much to his disillusionment, was barely considered in the government's rush to meet its sixty-day commitment. In his autobiography he describes the Cabinet debate of his proposal as "a sham": "the die had been cast before we met. The Prime Minister had neither the patience to consider genuine alternatives nor the ability to grasp the long-range significance of the issues."

Despite the problems, the Canada Pension Plan was introduced to the House of Commons in late 1964 and was passed to go into effect on January 1, 1966. Although the machinations had a serious effect on LaMarsh's future political career, she counted it as one of her major accomplishments. She was particularly proud of the fact that her colleagues agreed that the pension would be linked to the Consumer Price Index ("It meant we would not have to be forever adjusting pension benefits upward in the heat of a pre-election period") and that they agreed to bring down the age at which OAS benefits were paid — from age seventy to sixty-five over a five-year period.

So on January 1, 1966, the Canada and Quebec Pension Plans (C/QPP) came into being. The OAS Act was also amended to provide the monthly Guaranteed Income Supplement (GIS), added to OAS as a transitional measure to provide income-tested benefits for those with no or low C/QPP benefits. As well as these measures, some provinces also provide their own supplements to their residents based on income or needs tests.

At first the maximum for consumer price indexing was set at 2 percent a year. From 1968 to 1970 OAS benefits were indexed in the same way. In 1973 OAS indexing was changed to quarterly, and in 1974, the 2 percent C/QPP ceiling was removed although indexing was still annual. With the 1973-74 changes in public pensions, the government also fully indexed the federal public service plan to the Consumer Price Index. This development continues to draw the ire of private employees who depend on the generosity, not to mention the financial stability of employers for pension increases.

Whether or not Judy LaMarsh was happy with her contribution to the development of public pensions, there is no doubt that they have become a major source of pension income for Canadians.

A 1984 report of the National Council of Welfare said that federal and provincial programs account for 45.5 percent of the total income of elderly Canadians (sixty-five and older). That report also pointed out that government programs are most important to low-income seniors, accounting for almost all of their income.

In a 1990 report the council criticized Canada's income system for the elderly, saying it is too good to the rich, leaves many people in poverty and is unwise economically. The council was especially critical of the C/QPP, saying that although these plans pay out $7 billion a year to two million senior citizens, many recipients still receive federal income supplements to make ends meet. "We believe it is fundamentally wrong that a public pension program set up to cover the entire paid labour force is incapable of producing benefits large enough to keep most of its beneficiaries out of poverty," the report said.

The OAS is financed out of general government revenues, while the C/QPP is financed by equal contributions from employers and employees. While everyone age sixty-five or more receives the OAS pension, provided he or she meets the residence requirements, C/QPP benefits depend on covered earnings. The maximum benefit is set at 25 percent of the Average Industrial Composite (approximately $28,900 in 1990).

Some groups would like to double C/QPP benefits to 50 percent of the Average Industrial Composite. They believe that without an increase most Canadian will experience a decline in their standard of living when they retire because the private sector won't move voluntarily to ensure that more Canadians are covered by employer-sponsored plans.

Those who argue against doubling the C/QPP, mainly business groups, say it would cost too much. They estimate that to double benefits would require increasing the current contributions of workers and employers to as much as 20 percent of an individual's covered wages. As well, business, particularly the investment community, doesn't want the C/QPP to be expanded because it believes that, with such a large pool of funds available, the federal government would dominate the economy and reduce the flow of new capital.

However, whether C/QPP benefits are increased or not, it was inevitable that contributions would increase. The actuarial report that the federal Department of Insurance completed in June 1984 predicted that unless contributions increased to almost 11 percent of covered wages, the C/QPP fund would be exhausted by 2005, just by continuing benefits at 25 percent of the Average Industrial Wage. The report blamed the recent low birthrate, increasing life spans, and inflation for this situation.

At the same time, payments from the C/QPP were going out almost as fast as contributions were coming in. In 1982-83 contributions on behalf of workers were $4.4 billion, just $300 million more than needed to pay benefits. Although the C/QPP funds were not depleted, it was expected that the crunch could come in a few years when the number of people retiring from the labour force could exceed the number of young people entering the labour force.

Mainly as a result of these factors, the federal government announced early in 1986 that contributions would increase beginning on January 1, 1987.

While increasing contributions have helped stabilize the C/QPP, there are other suggestions for improving the operation of government plans. Some people have suggested that the age at which people receive government benefits should be raised from sixty-five to sixty-six or sixty-seven and that Old Age Security should be income-tested rather than universal. Proponents of this change argue that, although society has a responsibility to help those who have lost their earning power and security, it must do so justly: if an old person has a good income and security then it makes no sense to give that person money that would be better spent on those with more pressing problems. As a first attempt at dealing with this issue the federal government proposed limiting the indexation of Old Age Security benefits. However, such was the ire of the retired population that the government quickly retreated. In 1989 they took the more politically acceptable route of a tax "clawback" which effectively took the benefit away from individuals earning $50,000 or more.

An equally controversial issue has been that of pensions for homemakers. Homemakers are excluded from the C/QPP if they do not work outside the home because they do not contribute to the plan. The 1983 government task force on pensions proposed that the C/QPP be available to those who in any year worked only or mainly in the home to care for a spouse, a child under eighteen, or a dependent or infirm adult relative living in the home. For a person with no labour force earnings the pension would have been based on half the year's maximum pensionable earnings. Financing would have been through the existing C/QPP contribution structure, amended so that families who benefit from the pension pay the costs. Although the scheme was one of Brian Mulroney's promises in the 1984 election campaign, the Conservative government has not yet moved to implement it.

Everyone, it seems, has a scheme for improving the public pension system. Unfortunately, change is extremely difficult because control of pensions falls into both federal and provincial jurisdictions and the C/QPP cannot be changed without provincial approval. So far agreement has been reached on increasing the contributions from employers and employees and on splitting credits between married couples. However, when we consider the problems Judy LaMarsh faced in getting the CPP off the ground it is difficult to imagine that the path to amending it could be any less tortuous.

Private Plans

Building on the foundation provided by government pensions, the next layer in the Canadian pension system is provided by private or employer pension plans.

As we've seen, pure altruism was probably not the main reason employers began to provide retirement programs. Rewarding employees for long and faithful service was a by-product of more practical considerations. Getting rid of less productive, supposedly more accident-prone older workers supplied the impetus for establishing retirement plans in the late nineteenth century. Employers generally believed that "retiring the employee on a fair and properly determined pension is cheaper than keeping him on the payroll." Even unions were not completely benevolent in seeking pension plans for their members. For some unions, retirement was seen as a way of bringing in a new generation of workers and limiting numbers in industries where there were too many workers.

As work became more sophisticated there was another reason for employers to provide pension plans. Companies had to spend a good deal of money to train employees, and wanted a return on their investment. Pension plans were part of comprehensive fringe-benefits packages designed to attract good employees and, more important, to keep them.

As noted earlier, the transportation industry was among the first to provide retirement plans. In fact, Canada's Grand Trunk Railway established one of the first private pension plans in North America in 1874.

Most of us believe, rightly or wrongly, that civil servants have generous pension benefits. It's not surprising, then, to learn that the Public Service Superannuation Act in 1870 was actually the first formal pension plan in Canada. With the Pension Fund Societies Act in 1877 federally incorporated companies were allowed to establish pension-fund societies and pension plans spread into chartered banks.

Two pieces of federal legislation early in the twentieth century encouraged the further expansion of private pensions. In 1908 the Government Annuities Act provided a low-cost guaranteed vehicle for pension funding. Then, in 1919, the Income War Tax Act made employee pension contributions tax deductible.

In the 1920s a number of major industrial companies instituted plans, but the crash in 1929 virtually halted the introduction of employer-sponsored pension plans. The number of plans began to grow again as the economy recovered with the start of the Second World War.

During the next couple of decades, the number of pension plans grew dramatically, aided by favourable income tax rules. In 1945 there were only about 2,000 plans. This number increased to about 9,000 plans in 1960, to almost 14,000 in 1965, and to about 16,000 in 1970. By 1980 the number of plans had dipped to 14,500, but this figure has since rebounded, standing at a record 21,200 plans in 1988, covering an estimated 4.8 million workers in a variety of industries, or about 45 percent of the paid labour force in Canada.

Statistics, it's true, can be used to suit anyone's purpose. Critics of the private pension system point out that if public service and Crown corporation employees are subtracted from those figures it becomes clear that only about 31 percent of paid employees in private companies are covered by pension plans. Supporters of the private pension system argue that the total labour force includes many people who would not be eligible for coverage by pension plans — they are too young or too old, they work part time, they are unemployed, they are self-employed, or they have elected not to join the pension plan. Supporters maintain that if the total labour force didn't include these people then the figure would show that 75 percent to 80 percent of the labour force is covered by private plans.

Nonetheless, there is no doubt that a section of the work force is not being reached by private pension plans.

Those who are not covered are employed mainly in small businesses, retail stores, the professions, small agencies, and contracting companies.

Perhaps the most sobering statistic comes from the National Council of Welfare. In its report in 1990 the council concluded that most elderly Canadians have modest incomes and that even many recipients of C/QPP benefits still receive federal income supplements to make ends meet because they do not have other sources of retirement income. About 24.4 percent of households headed by senior citizens lived in poverty in 1986, according to Statistics Canada. The Canadian Council on Social Development put the figure at 41 percent.

Until the 1960s, private pension plans were monitored by Revenue Canada, which also stipulated the maximum contributions and benefits which were permitted. In the early 1960s, however, the provinces decided they should be more involved. Ontario drafted a Portable Pensions Act which set minimum standards to be met by private pension plans. Ontario wanted to ensure that employees understood what they were entitled to and that they would receive the benefits they had been promised. A 1963 draft of the Act included requirements for mandatory minimum pension plans. This feature was dropped later when the Canada Pension Plan was introduced.

The Pension Benefits Act of Ontario was effective January 1, 1965. Other provinces followed with similar legislation. For more than 20 years the rules governing private plans remained largely unchanged.

From 1965 to 1985 private industry's role in improving the lot of elderly Canadians was a hotly debated issue. Critics pointed to the low number of workers covered and the inadequacy of retirement incomes from private plans. There was much discussion about how to protect pensioners' incomes against inflation, how to ensure that workers who change jobs frequently can have adequate pensions, and how to provide better incomes for elderly women. Because of the political implications of many of the issues, both the federal government and the provinces produced a multitude of studies, commissions, and papers.

Finally, in 1986, Ottawa and the provinces announced changes to deal with a number of the issues. The plight of elderly women was relieved by splitting C/QPP benefits between spouses on marriage breakdown and altering private plans so that spouses are entitled to survivors' pensions when a plan member dies. To help workers who change jobs frequently, "vesting" rules were changed in several jurisdictions. The main outstanding issues are how to provide coverage through the private sector for more workers and how to deal with the effects of inflation.

Inflation protection continues to be one of the thorniest issues. Business supports the current system whereby many employers make voluntary adjustments for inflation when a company's finances permit. However, most companies reject the idea of a compulsory approach that would dictate increases based on the Consumer Price Index. They argue that this approach wouldn't take into account a company's financial state. A company could be forced to increase pensions even though it didn't have enough money available.

During the years since provincial legislation governing private pension plans was first introduced, a new philosophy has emerged. In the 1960s pensions were supposedly granted out of the generosity of the employer, to provide retirement security for long-service employees. Now pension plans are expected to meet a variety of social needs and have come to be regarded as an employee's "deferred pay." The ultimate extension of this philosophy would be a system whereby all pension plan members had an inalienable right to all contributions made on their behalf. Canada has not yet reached that point.

Personal Financial Planning

The third leg of the pension stool is personal savings. Societies' perception of older people has changed dramatically since the Industrial Revolution. At the same time the extended family has been replaced by the nuclear family. Although the government stepped in to provide basic income to those over age sixty-five through OAS and the C/QPP, it was still left up to the individual to make some provisions for his or her own retirement. The theory is that personal financial planning for retirement allows people to establish their own priorities based on their own economic circumstances.

Personal saving can take many forms. For many people, buying a home is the only investment they are likely to make. A much smaller number have enough money to invest in savings bonds, guaranteed investment certificates, mortgages, or other riskier vehicles such as mutual funds and common stocks. For the average person, however, saving for retirement is usually pre-empted by mortgage payments, orthodontist's bills, university tuition, perhaps a new car. The list can seem endless and retirement is always a long way down on it.

For more and more people Registered Retirement Savings Plans (RRSPs) are offering an opportunity to put aside money for retirement. The advantage of RRSPs, of course, is that they allow people to save on income taxes — for as long as the savings plans are not cashed in. Tax-sheltered RRSPs were introduced in 1957, yet it was not until the 1970s that they attained the popularity they have now.

The purpose of an RRSP is to provide retirement income. The contributor is supposed to purchase an "annuity" or a Registered Retirement Income Fund (RRIF) with the proceeds. An annuity involves a series of regular payments; so, in essence, the contributor pays himself or herself a monthly income out of the money saved on the plan. Payments begin as early as age sixty and they must begin no later than the end of the year in which you celebrate your seventy-first birthday. A RRIF is a more flexible alternative under which payments are made for a fixed period of years. We discuss RRIFs in more detail in part IV. Of course, there are government-imposed limits on how much can be used as a tax shelter each year. From their slow start RRSPs have grown enormously — contributions in 1987 alone were over $9 billion.

The National Council of Welfare argued in its 1984 report that people with higher earnings (above the average wage) are more likely to have RRSPs "or otherwise set aside enough savings to make an appreciable contribution to their retirement income." The council continued this line of argument in its 1990 report when it attacked federal plans to raise the maximum contribution to retirement savings plans by 1995 to $15,500 a year on earnings as large as $86,111 — a limit the council calls "excessively generous to employees who are already rich by any standard." Despite the council's arguments, it seems that, with the marketing thrust of the financial institutions and the popularity of RRSPs that this has generated, far more Canadians in the future are likely to have retirement income generated from RRSPs.

Undoubtedly, as the "baby boom" generation grows older its priorities will shift naturally from establishing households and raising families to preparing for retirement. With this shift will come increasing emphasis on personal savings. It is significant that annual contributions to RRSPs in Canada for 1977 through 1987 grew at a compound annual growth rate of 14.3 percent. This exceeded the growth in other forms of pension savings and the growth in general economic activity. Such voluntary pension arrangements are a vital and growing source of long-term investment capital.

We believe individuals should continue to take some initiative in planning for their own retirement. And we support any attempts to upgrade voluntary individual-based pension arrangements to make them more attractive and affordable for all Canadians.

*   *   *

Now that you have a basic idea of where your retirement income will come from, let's take a closer look at the details of how pension plans operate.

Please meet Harry and Alice March. Harry was born in 1947 and Alice in 1949. Harry will earn $44,000 in 1991 as supervisor of claims processing with a major Canadian life insurance company. When Maria and David, their two teenagers, were both in school full time, Alice went back to work as assistant to the vice-president of a small manufacturing company. The couple are using her salary to pay their mortgage and to save for university for Maria and David. Harry and Alice know they are members of their companies' pension plans and that they will probably be eligible for pensions from the Canada Pension Plan and Old Age Security. Harry has also been thinking about putting a bit of money into a personal Registered Retirement Savings Plan. But, like most of us, Harry and Alice have only a vague understanding of the details of their pension plans. More and more, retirement planning is a topic of conversation among their friends and associates. Most of them are as concerned as the Marches. How much income can they expect when they retire? What else can they do to ensure they will be able to enjoy financially secure retirement years?

Let's look first at government pension plans and how they will affect Harry and Alice and their friends and associates.

PART II

GOVERNMENT PROGRAMS

2

Alphabet Soup

*There is only a certain sized cake to be divided
up, and if a lot of people want a larger slice they
can only take it from others who would, in terms
of real income, have a smaller one.*

Sir Stafford Cripps

CPP, QPP, OAS, GIS . . . pension programs sponsored by the government resemble alphabet soup, which perhaps makes them seem more complicated than they really are. With the help of the Marches, we can see how these programs operate.

Of the government-sponsored pension programs the Old Age Security program is the easiest to understand. Both Harry and Alice will receive the full pension when they reach age sixty-five because they have lived in Canada for the required number of years. Residence in Canada is the only test you have to pass to receive the full pension. If you live in Canada for periods that total at least forty years between your eighteenth birthday and your sixty-fifth birthday you will be eligible for the full pension. This means that you could have lived or worked outside Canada for up to seven years and still qualify.

Harry was born in Canada, has always lived here, and doesn't expect to live anywhere else (although he and Alice have talked about how nice it would be to spend their winters in Florida when they retire). Although Alice was born in England, she will qualify for the full OAS pension, too, because she immigrated to Canada with her parents when she was seventeen and has lived here ever since. Until July 1, 1977, you could also qualify for the full OAS if you had lived in Canada for at least ten years without interruption immediately before you applied for your pension. If you were at least twenty-five on July 1, 1977, you could choose to be covered by the old rule. This is what happened to Alice's father.

Alice's father turned sixty-five in November 1986. Because he was forty-four when he came to Canada as a landed immigrant he didn't have the required forty years of residence. However, as he lived here in 1977 and was over twenty-five on that date, he qualified under the old rule. He is a Canadian citizen and he had lived in Canada for at least ten years (in his case actually twenty-one years) immediately before he applied for his pension. Alice's father had become a Canadian citizen. If he had been a landed immigrant or if he were in Canada on a visitor's permit he would still have been eligible for the full pension.

If you have lived outside Canada as a member of the armed forces or because you work for the government you would probably be considered a resident of Canada even while you were outside the country.

Many people in Canada will be eligible for the full pension either because they pass the forty-year residence test or because they were twenty-five or over on July 1, 1977, and qualify under the old rules. However, some people receive a part pension. If you don't meet the requirements we outlined above, you may qualify for a part pension if you live in Canada now and have lived in Canada for at least ten years between your eighteenth birthday and your sixty-fifth birthday. Your part pension would be calculated as one-fortieth (remember forty years of residence is normally required to qualify) of the full pension for each year you have lived in Canada up to forty years.

This was the case with Alice's uncle. Alice's Uncle George was born in England and immigrated to Canada when he was thirty-nine. George's wife wasn't happy here so when he was forty-five they went back to England. While back in England George made a bit of money from a small business he sold. When his wife died four years ago, he decided to come back to Canada and live with Alice's father who is also a widower. George will be sixty-five in

1992 and will have only eleven years' total residence in Canada. He'll receive eleven-fortieths of the full pension.

Even former residents who no longer live in Canada can qualify for a part pension. They don't even have to return to Canada to collect it. Anyone who lived in Canada as a citizen, a landed immigrant, or on a visitor's permit for at least twenty years after his or her eighteenth birthday could qualify.

If you are within a few years of retirement and are not sure if you meet the residence test for OAS, contact the federal government's Income Security Programs office near you for information.

To make sure you receive your OAS as soon as you reach age sixty-five you should apply at least six months before your sixty-fifth birthday. You can pick up an application form at most post offices or receive one by mail by contacting your nearest Income Security Programs office. Because the government needs six months to process your application, we suggest you get your application form about eight months before your sixty-fifth birthday. This will allow enough time to check any information that is required and to gather together the necessary documents.

As well as the completed application form, you will need proof of your age. A birth certificate or baptismal certificate is best. If you don't have either one, check with the Income Security Programs office for a list of other documents that are acceptable. Your Social Insurance Number is also required on the form. If you don't have one you will have to contact your nearest Employment and Immigration office to get one. Similarly, if you were not born in Canada, you will have to provide proof of citizenship. If you don't have a Certificate of Citizenship, a Naturalization Certificate, or a Canadian Immigration Identification Record you will have to contact Employment and Immigration for evidence of your residence status in Canada. As you can see, it could take several months to collect all the necessary documents.

Normally, if you apply at least six months before your sixty-fifth birthday and your application is straightforward, you should begin receiving your monthly cheques as soon as you turn sixty-five. However, if your case is complicated and your application is not processed by your sixty-fifth birthday, the government will pay you retroactively for up to twelve months once your application is approved.

The OAS pension is paid to every Canadian aged sixty-five — male or female; married or single; healthy, sick, or disabled. Even if you continue working beyond age sixty-five you will still receive the OAS at age sixty-five. However, when you die, the OAS ends. There are no survivor benefits; your spouse will probably be receiving his or her own OAS.

The OAS is currently adjusted every three months in line with increases in the Consumer Price Index. The following table shows how the OAS has increased over the past two years and how it might increase over the next few years (assuming the Consumer Price Index increases by 5 percent each year).

Year	Monthly Pension at January 1
1989	$323.28
1990	340.07
1991	357.07
1992	374.93
1993	393.67
1994	413.36
1995	434.03

The OAS is paid out of general tax revenue. You don't contribute directly. Therefore, you will still receive the pension no matter how many times you change jobs before age sixty-five or whether you work for someone else or are self-employed.

Remember that Harry and Alice were thinking of wintering in Florida when they retire. If they do, they will still receive their full OAS pensions, but of course because they'll be paid in Canadian dollars.

Not everyone who leaves Canada at age sixty-five will necessarily receive the OAS. If you have not lived in Canada for twenty years between age eighteen and sixty-five you will only receive your OAS for six months after you leave Canada. If you have lived outside Canada in a country that has a reciprocal social-security agreement with Canada then you may use this time to help establish the twenty-year requirement. However, it will not affect the amount of pension you receive.

In Chapter 18 we discuss in more detail the question of what happens to your Old Age Security pension if you live outside Canada for part of your working life.

Your OAS pension will be paid to you whether you live at home or in an institution. But what if you are too sick or disabled to manage your own affairs? Health and Welfare Canada recognizes that this could happen. In such a case it would appoint a person or an agency to act on your behalf. This person or agency would have to account for the money it received and spent on your behalf every year, as long as it looks after your affairs.

As we have said, the OAS pension is paid to everyone at age sixty-five who satisfies the residence requirement. In only one case could the pension be paid earlier. It could be paid to a spouse beginning at age sixty. This special circumstance applies if you are receiving OAS, if your spouse meets the residence requirements for OAS, and if your combined incomes are very low. The amount your spouse would receive would depend on how many years of residence he or she had and the total of your combined incomes. Naturally, this Spouse's Allowance would only be paid until your spouse reaches age sixty-five because at that point he or she would be receiving the OAS pension.

Old Age Security is a program of the federal government and the federal government decides how the program will operate. We saw in Chapter 1 the many changes the OAS has undergone since it was introduced in 1927. Recently we have seen more changes.

During the 1984 election campaign Brian Mulroney promised that the universality of social programs was a "sacred trust" and would never be tampered with. However, some people began to question whether the country could continue to afford universality.

Some experts suggest that one way to save money is to raise the age at which OAS benefits are paid. It is estimated that raising the qualifying age to sixty-six would save about $1 billion a year (at 1986 expenditure levels) and raising it to sixty-seven would save about $2 billion a year. The argument for raising the qualifying age rests on the idea that, in 1966, when the OAS qualifying age was lowered, life expectancies were below what they are now.

Despite their assurances, in May of 1985 the federal government proposed to index Old Age Security to inflation only in excess of 3%. This change would have been phased in over a five-year period and was seen by many as the beginning of the end of universality.

Protests grew. Groups like the United Seniors of Ontario and even business associations joined in. Finally, on June 19, at a big demonstration on Parliament Hill, Brian Mulroney was confronted by sixty-three-year-old Solange Denis. She said he had mislead them when he promised to protect social security payments from inflation. "You lied to us," she said, "so it's goodbye Charlie Brown!"

Soon afterwards the proposals were shelved, but only after the seniors of Canada realized the collective power they could now command.

What seemed inevitable was that sooner or later OAS payments would be taxed away from those over a certain income level. In the federal budget of April, 1989, the Conservative government announced that henceforth individuals with "income" over $50,000 would have to pay back all or some of any OAS and Family Allowance benefits received in the year by way of a special tax. The special tax is known as the "clawback". The clawback continues to be debated in personal financial columns in business newspapers and magazines, but it seems unlikely that it will be changed.

3

Where You Come In

*I advise you to go on living solely to enrage those
who are paying your annuity.*

Voltaire

IN ADDITION TO THE OAS, most working Canadians, including
Harry and Alice March, will also receive retirement income from
the Canada or Quebec Pension Plan. Any Canadian who works
and contributes to the C/QPP is eligible for a pension. (In Chapter 1
when we outlined the history of how the CPP started we indicated
that Quebec had some ideas of its own. Although the Quebec Pension Plan operates under a different name, the two plans are virtually the same. We will use "Canada Pension Plan [CPP]" to refer to
both plans and where there are differences we will note them.)

The Canada Pension Plan came into effect on January 1, 1966,
and almost every Canadian who begins working after his or her
eighteenth birthday becomes a member. There are a few exceptions. Migratory workers in such occupations as farming, fishing,
trapping, hunting, and logging don't belong if they work fewer
than twenty-five days a year for the same employer or earn less
than $250 a year from the same employer. Generally, members of
religious orders who have taken vows of perpetual poverty do not
belong, and exchange teachers who come from another country to
teach in Canada are not required to join the Canada Pension Plan.

Probably, when you started your first job, your employer asked
you to fill out an application form for a Social Insurance Number
(SIN). The contributions made to the CPP on your behalf and the

benefits you will eventually receive are related to your earnings. The government's computers keep track of your earnings from age eighteen to age sixty-five by using your SIN.

Both you and your employer contribute to the CPP every year you are working. If you are self-employed you contribute both the employee's share and the employer's share. From January 1, 1966, to January 1, 1987, the contribution rate was 3.6 percent of eligible earnings. You contributed 1.8 percent and your employer contributed 1.8 percent. In 1985 the government realized that the CPP would run out of money to pay future pensions, unless contribution rates were increased. Beginning January 1, 1987, the rate increases each year by 0.2 percent (0.1 percent from you, 0.1 percent from your employer) until January 1, 1992. On January 1, 1992, the contribution rate will be increased by 0.15 percent (0.075 percent from you and 0.075 percent from your employer) each year until 2011. By then the total contribution will be 7.6 percent. You will contribute 3.8 percent and your employer will contribute 3.8 percent. If you take a close look at your paycheque, you will see where you employer has deducted your CPP contribution. Your contributions are deductible for income tax purposes.

You and your employer do not necessarily contribute on your total earnings. There is a maximum yearly contribution. It is based on the difference between what are called the Year's Basic Exemption (YBE) and the Year's Maximum Pensionable Earnings (YMPE). If you earn less than the Year's Basic Exemption in any year you do not contribute to the CPP. If you earn more than the Year's Maximum Pensionable Earnings in any year you contribute only on the amount you earn between the YBE and the YMPE. The table on page 31 shows rates during the last twenty years of the CPP.

When you begin receiving pension benefits the amount you receive will be based on your earnings. Your monthly pension is calculated as 25 percent of your average monthly pensionable earnings. The CPP takes your total pensionable earnings over the years you worked (total pensionable earnings will be either your total actual earnings or total YMPEs, whichever is less). It will adjust your earnings to bring them to current values as a way of protecting you from the full effect of inflation. These adjusted earnings

Calendar Year	Year's Basic Exemption	Year's Maximum Pensionable Earnings	Maximum Employee Contribution	Maximum Employer Contribution
1971	$ 600	$ 5,400	$ 86.40	$ 86.40
1972	600	5,500	88.20	88.20
1973	600	5,600	90.00	90.00
1974	700	6,600	106.20	106.20
1975	700	7,400	120.60	120.60
1976	800	8,300	135.00	135.00
1977	900	9,300	151.20	151.20
1978	1,000	10,400	169.20	169.20
1979	1,100	11,700	190.80	190.80
1980	1,300	13,100	212.40	212.40
1981	1,400	14,700	239.40	239.40
1982	1,600	16,500	268.20	268.20
1983	1,800	18,500	300.60	300.60
1984	2,000	20,800	338.40	338.40
1985	2,300	23,400	379.80	379.80
1986	2,500	25,800	419.40	419.40
1987	2,500	25,900	444.60	444.60
1988	2,600	26,500	478.00	478.00
1989	2,700	27,700	525.00	525.00
1990	2,800	28,900	574.20	574.20

are used to calculate your average monthly earnings for the entire period you contributed.

To protect your pension further, the CPP will not include periods in which you had no or low earnings — such periods may total up to 15 percent of your contributory period. For example, if you attended university for three years and worked only during the summer, you would have contributed to the CPP, but your earnings were probably quite low during those years.

The calculations are probably easier to understand if we look at a particular case. Harry March is fairly typical. When he graduated from high school in June 1965 he went to work in the office of a small manufacturing company in his home town. The Canada Pension Plan became law in May that year but the plan wasn't implemented until January 1, 1966. Although Harry was eighteen when he started working, he didn't join the CPP until it came into effect the following January 1.

Just before he turned twenty-one, Harry decided it was time to move to the city. He had an aunt in Toronto who offered to rent him a room. So he quit his job and, like many other young people, went off to Toronto to seek his fortune. After only a few weeks of job hunting he was hired by an insurance company as a trainee in the claims department. He has been with them ever since. Harry has been contributing to the CPP since it started. He expects to continue working until age sixty-five. If he does, he will have contributed to the CPP for forty-six years. As his salary has always been at least equal to the YMPE he will be entitled to a full CPP benefit when he retires at age sixty-five.

But what about Alice? She is two years younger than Harry and she didn't work outside the home from the time she became pregnant with David until David was nine years old and Maria was seven — a period of almost ten years.

When Alice came to Canada at age seventeen she went into Grade 12 at the local high school. At the end of that year she decided to go to secretarial school for a year. Then, at age nineteen, she began to look for a job. Alice joined the typing pool at a large insurance company. She was an excellent typist and through the company's job-posting program she moved up fairly quickly. Three years later, when she was twenty-two, Alice became secretary to the vice-president of the claims department.

Harry was training to be a claims adjuster in the same department. They started dating. Two years later they were married. The insurance company didn't want a married couple working in the same department so they moved Alice into a clerical job in the personnel department. She had been there only six months when she learned that she was two months pregnant.

Let's look at Alice's CPP history. She was nineteen when she began working and the CPP had been in effect for two years. As soon as she joined the insurance company she had to apply for her Social Insurance Number and she began contributing to the CPP. When she quit working she had belonged to the CPP for five and a half years. She stayed at home with the children for almost ten years. When she went back to work as assistant to the president of a small manufacturing firm she began contributing to the CPP again. That was seven years ago. Alice plans to continue working until Harry retires, at which point she will be sixty-three. If she does she will have contributed to the CPP for a total of 33.5 years. Unlike Harry, Alice has never been paid as much as the YMPE so her pension will be less than the maximum which Harry will receive.

As we said, Harry plans to retire at age sixty-five and Alice at sixty-three. Until the rules were changed on January 1, 1987, Harry would have received his CPP benefits but Alice would have had to wait until she was sixty-five. Now, however, you can begin receiving a pension as early as age sixty, but that pension will be "actuarially" adjusted to take into account the fact that you are receiving it early and that, therefore, you will be paid longer than if you had retired at age sixty-five.

What if you continue working past age sixty-five? Then you have a choice. You can receive your CPP pension based on your contributions to age sixty-five. If you do, you cannot continue to contribute to the plan. Alternatively, you can decide to wait a few years before beginning to receive your pension. You can contribute until your seventieth birthday. After that you can no longer make contributions. Again your pension will be actuarially adjusted. If you decide to receive your pension sometime between age sixty-five and seventy, you will receive a larger pension than you would have at age sixty-five.

The adjustment factor that will be used will be 0.5 percent for each month you are under or over age sixty-five. If you retire at age sixty you will receive 70 percent of the pension you would have received at age sixty-five. If, however, you choose age seventy to begin receiving your CPP pension, you will receive 130 percent of the pension you would have received at age sixty-five.

Because Alice wants to receive her CPP pension when she is sixty-three (twenty-four months early) she will receive 88 percent of the pension she would have received at sixty-five (100 percent − (0.5 percent × 24 months) = 100 percent − 12 percent).

Death Benefits

The CPP provides other benefits besides retirement income. If you have been contributing long enough and your survivors meet the age requirements, the CPP also provides death benefits if you die. Three types of benefits are paid: a lump sum; a monthly pension to your spouse; and a monthly pension for each surviving dependent child.

In order for the death benefits to be paid you have to have contributed to the CPP for either one-third of the calendar years in which you are eligible to contribute or for ten calendar years, whichever is less (but for a minimum of three calendar years).

Does that seem a bit confusing? Well, what would happen if Harry or Alice had been killed in a car accident on the way home from work in September 1990? Harry, as we saw earlier, has been contributing to the CPP since it started on January 1, 1966. By September 1990 he had been contributing for 23.66 years. No problem here. Alice would receive benefits. (We'll figure out how much later.)

But what if Alice had been killed? Would Harry have received benefits? Alice had worked for five and a half years, stayed at home for almost ten years, and has been back at work for about seven years. Alice was eligible to join the CPP when she was eighteen. Now she is forty-two. She has been eligible to contribute to the CPP for twenty-four years. She has actually contributed for about twelve and a half years. Not only does she satisfy the ten-year requirement, but twelve and one-half years is more than one third of twenty years, so Harry should receive benefits.

The lump-sum death benefit payment is supposed to be six times a person's monthly retirement pension. If you had not retired yet, Health and Welfare would calculate a monthly pension for you as if you had been retired at the time of your death. However, there is a limit — 10 percent of the Year's Maximum Pensionable Earnings. To give you an idea of how this works, let's consider Harry's father.

Harry's father retired in January 1985. He had been contributing to the CPP since it started and qualified for the maximum pension which was $435.42 in 1985. Unfortunately, Harry's father suffered a massive coronary in September 1985 and died suddenly. The death benefit that was paid to Harry's mother was not 6 × $435.42 or $2,612.52 but was $2,340, the maximum for 1985. The table below shows the maximum lump-sum death benefit for each of the last twenty years, up to and including 1990.

Year	Maximum Lump-Sum Death Benefit	Year	Maximum Lump-Sum Death Benefit
1971	$ 540	1981	1,470
1972	550	1982	1,650
1973	560	1983	1,850
1974	660	1984	2,080
1975	740	1985	2,340
1976	830	1986	2,580
1977	930	1987	2,590
1978	1,040	1988	2,650
1979	1,170	1989	2,770
1980	1,310	1990	2,890

Whether or not your surviving spouse and children will receive CPP benefits and how much they will receive depend on their ages and their circumstances. Let's look at the spouse's pension first. Harry's mother receives the maximum spouse's pension because she is over age sixty-five. Her pension is 60 percent of what Harry's father would have received as a pension. She receives the maximum because she never worked outside their home and so has no CPP pension of her own.

If she had been receiving her own CPP pension, the amount would be adjusted. Until January 1, 1987, she would have received 60 percent of her monthly pension plus 60 percent of the current value of Harry's father's pension. Now a surviving spouse receives his or her own CPP benefit plus the survivor benefit to a total equivalent to one pension at the maximum rate. This change should help older widows who often had low earnings and thus low CPP pensions of their own.

Now let's go back to Harry and Alice. If one of them died, the amount of the benefit the survivor would receive would be different from the benefit Harry's mother receives because they are under age sixty-five. This is also a situation in which the benefits they receive would differ depending on whether they contributed to the Canada Pension Plan or the Quebec Pension Plan. If Harry or Alice were to die, the survivor would receive a pension because he or she is over age thirty-five. There are several rules which govern the amount of the monthly pension they would be entitled to, however.

Because Harry and Alice contribute to the CPP, let's look at benefits under the CPP first. The maximum monthly pension to a surviving spouse is a flat amount plus 37.5 percent of the monthly pension the deceased spouse had earned. The maximum is paid to anyone over age forty-five or to anyone who has dependent children or is disabled. Because Harry and Alice have dependent children they would be eligible for the maximum benefits under the formula. Reduced monthly pensions are paid to surviving spouses who are between the ages of thirty-five and forty-five if they have no dependent children or are not disabled. The maximum is reduced by 1/120 for each month by which the surviving spouse is under age forty-five. Let's say Harry and Alice had no dependants and Alice died. Harry's pension would be reduced by 12/120 or 10 percent of what he would receive now with dependants. If a surviving spouse is under age thirty-five, has no dependants and is not disabled he or she does not receive a surviving spouse's pension. Health and Welfare Canada assumes that these people would have "little difficulty in finding employment and may remarry."

In Quebec the benefits to surviving spouses between age thirty-five and sixty-five are more generous than for those who are over age sixty-five. The difference results from the fact that the flat amount that Quebec uses in calculating benefits is higher than that used under the CPP. The flat amount in Quebec also depends on the age of the surviving spouse. It is highest for those age fifty-five to sixty-four and somewhat lower for those under age fifty-five. As with the CPP, QPP benefits are reduced for spouses under forty-five who have no dependants and are not disabled. No pension is paid to anyone under age thirty-five if the survivor has no dependants and is not disabled.

The CPP and QPP also pay orphan's benefits for each dependent child who is under age eighteen or under age twenty-five if attending school full time. Under the QPP the benefit is $29 for each dependent child. Under the CPP the amount of the benefit changes each year. This is one of the areas that was improved as a result of changes to the C/QPP that came into effect on January 1, 1987. Previously, if both parents were contributing to the CPP and died, the orphan or orphans received the same amount they would have received if only one parent had died. If Harry and Alice were to die together in a car accident, Maria and David would each receive a benefit for each parent. Of course, if Alice had not contributed to the CPP, Maria and David would receive only one benefit. New legislation has also changed another point about survivor benefits. Until January 1, 1987, benefits to a survivor ended when the survivor remarried. Now benefits will continue if the survivor remarries. What happens if your spouse died in 1980 and you remarried in 1985 and lost your survivor pension? Your pension should have begun again in 1987 but you would not have received retroactive benefits for 1985 and 1986. Contact your nearest Income Security Programs office for information on how to apply for reinstatement of benefits.

Disability Benefits

So far we have talked about the benefits that are paid if you have been working and contributing to the CPP. But what would happen if you became disabled and couldn't work?

To receive the disability pension you must satisfy certain requirements. You must be under age sixty-five, your disability must be severe and prolonged, and you must have contributed to the CPP or QPP for a minimum period. This is another rule that was eased on January 1, 1987. Now you can receive a disability pension if you had contributed to the CPP for at least two of the last three years or five of the last ten years. A severe disability means that you can't work in any substantially gainful occupation. A prolonged disability means your disability is expected to last indefinitely or is likely to result in your death.

You must submit medical evidence from your family doctor. But the decision as to whether or not you will receive disability benefits is made by a "disability determination board." The board may ask you to undertake another medical examination. If so, the CPP will pay any cost.

The CPP also requires you to undergo "reasonable" rehabilitation measures. It can cut off benefits if you refuse a medical examination or suggested rehabilitation measures. The rules for eligibility for benefits are not as strict now as they were before January 1, 1987; on that date the benefits for the disabled were increased.

Similar to survivor benefits, the disability pension consists of a flat amount plus 75 percent of the current value of your monthly retirement benefit. This means your benefit is calculated as if you had retired on the day you begin receiving your disability pension. As of January 1, 1987, the flat amount was raised under the CPP to bring it up to the level stipulated under the QPP which until then had been more generous.

A disability pension usually begins four months after your disability begins. If you begin receiving a disability pension you no longer contribute to the CPP as long as you are receiving the pension.

The CPP also provides benefits for your dependent children if you are disabled. The amount is the same as for orphans. Dependent children must be unmarried, under age eighteen, or under twenty-five if attending school full time.

A disability pension ends when you recover, die, or reach age sixty-five, whichever occurs first. If you reach age sixty-five the disability pension would be replaced by a retirement pension. When you die your surviving spouse and dependent children would receive the survivor benefits we discussed earlier.

Your Spouse and the CPP

We've discussed the benefits that are available to your spouse when you die or become disabled. On January 1, 1978, the CPP recognized that more and more Canadian marriages were ending in divorce. The CPP decided it would divide equally the CPP credits earned by both you and your spouse during your years of marriage. However, you or your spouse had to ask for this to be done. Now, when a marriage ends in divorce, "credit splitting," designed to provide some financial protection for the spouse who worked in the home or who had lower earnings during the marriage, is automatic.

Let's suppose Harry and Alice get a divorce in 1992. Although Alice is back in the workforce now, she hasn't contributed to the CPP for as long as Harry. The pension she earns by 1992 will be less than the CPP pension Harry has earned by then. The split will be made no matter what property settlement is made between Alice and Harry.

The period for which the credits are divided begins in January of the year the marriage began and ends in December of the year before the marriage ended or of the year before the one in which the couple stopped living together. A spouse who separates or whose common-law relationship ends can also apply to split CPP credits.

In 1978, the CPP also added a child-care drop-out provision. This allows for months of low or zero earnings while a person was caring for a child under age seven (and receiving Family Allowances for the child) to be dropped from their pension calculation, in addition to the 15 percent drop-out described earlier. In Alice's case this means that she will be able to drop out the years from the time David was born until Maria reached age seven — about nine years. Let's compare Alice's pension without dropping out those years and with the drop-out feature.

Alice's potential contributory period was from 1967 (when she was eighteen) to 2014 (age sixty-five): a total of forty-seven years. Her actual contributions were made from age nineteen to age twenty-four and a half and from seven years ago to the present. She expects to contribute until age sixty-three. Her total expected contributory period will be thirty-three and a half years. Her 15 percent drop-out is seven years. Her child-care drop-out is nine years. Her potential contributory period is thus cut back to thirty-one years. If Alice had always earned above the YMPE she would be entitled to a full CPP benefit.

As of this writing, homemakers are excluded from the CPP. However, a homemakers' pension was recommended by the 1983 government task force and was promised by the Conservative party in the 1984 election campaign. Since then it has moved quietly to the back burner.

Homemakers are excluded now if they do not work outside the home because they do not contribute to the plan. The proposal is that the pension be available to those who in any year work mainly in the home to care for a spouse, a child under eighteen, or a dependent or infirm adult relative living in the home. For a person with no labour-force earnings the pension would be based on half the Year's Maximum Pensionable Earnings. Financing would be through the current CPP contribution structure, amended so that families who benefit from the pension pay the cost.

The arguments against such a homemakers' pension are generally concerned with the inequities that could result. The examples cited include the fact that a millionaire's spouse with no independent earnings could hire a full-time single housekeeper and still be eligible for a homemakers' pension that would likely be larger than the housekeeper's C/QPP retirement cheques. Similarly, a low-income working widow with children, through her C/QPP contributions, would help pay for the subsidized pension of an affluent widow who stays home to raise a family. Both women would receive the same benefits on reaching retirement age. At issue, also, is whether the idea of a homemakers' pension fully recognizes the increasing participation of women in the labour force.

Inflation Protection and Portability

Two of the major issues discussed in the past fifteen years of pension debate were inflation protection and portability.

Will your CPP pension be protected from inflation? The answer is yes. All benefits from the Canada Pension Plan are adjusted each January 1 in line with the Consumer Price Index.

As well, the C/QPP are fully portable across Canada. This means that no matter how many times you change employers and no matter where you have lived, you will be eligible for benefits based on your earnings and contributions.

If You Are Self-Employed

Canadians who have their own businesses, or are otherwise self-employed, must belong to the CPP. However, if you are one of these people, you must contribute the amount required each year, both from the employee and from the employer. You should make your contributions quarterly.

Who Looks After the Assets?

Currently about ten million Canadians contribute to the Canada Pension Plan and three million contribute to the Quebec Pension Plan. What happens to all of that money?

Obviously some of it is paid out to retired Canadians. But a great deal of money has accumulated in the CPP fund because, in the early years, the contribution rate was more than what was required. Most of this money that wasn't needed to pay benefits has been loaned to the provinces. (We'll discuss the situation in Quebec later.) The provinces then use the money to provide economic and social programs. The amount the provinces can borrow is related to the amount of the contributions coming into the fund from its residents.

The CPP has been criticized for lending its money to the provinces for two reasons. First, it has lent the money at very attractive interest rates. Second, it is doubtful that the provinces will ever be able to pay back the money. The CPP argues that it lends to the provinces at rates only slightly lower than the current market — the rate at which the federal government borrows funds. Further, the argument runs, if the provinces paid market rates, the fund would only be larger now by an extra three months' worth of benefit payments and the CPP would still be facing a financial crisis. On the issue of whether the provinces can pay back the money, the CPP points out that several provinces have set up special funds to make repayments.

However, it is clear that the CPP fund was coming to a crunch as it anticipated the aging of the "baby boom" generation. That's the main reason contribution rates are increasing. Based on CPP projections, if contributions aren't increased now, then our children and grandchildren will be faced with huge increases to pay for our benefits. We indicated earlier how the rates will increase over the next twenty-five years.

The rules which govern the CPP are made at the federal level. However, any changes must be approved by at least two-thirds of those provinces with two-thirds of the population of Canada.

The Régie des rentes du Québec administers the Quebec Pension Plan. Contributions are collected by the Quebec Department of Revenue and turned over to the Régie which keeps what is needed to pay current benefits and administer expenditures. The remaining funds are deposited with the Caisse de dépôt et placement du Québec.

Public Relations

Health and Welfare Canada has launched a campaign to ensure that Canadians are informed about their contributions to and the benefits they may receive from the Canada Pension Plan. If you haven't already, you will soon receive a personalized statement from Health and Welfare. It will tell you what your eligible earnings have been. It will also show death and disability benefits available to you or your dependants.

Health and Welfare Canada intends to distribute these statements every three or four years. In the meantime, you can apply for a statement once in any twelve-month period. An "Application for Statement of Earnings" form is available from your local Income Security Programs office.

4

Have The Means and Fail the Test

*Four spectres haunt the poor—old age,
accident, sickness and unemployment.*

David Lloyd George

WHEN THE CANADA PENSION PLAN WAS INTRODUCED in 1966, the Guaranteed Income Supplement (GIS) was also instituted. It was to be a transitional measure for Canadians with no or low CPP benefits. The GIS is a means-tested pension, available to people who receive Old Age Security and have little or no other income. GIS benefits are payable tax-free to eligible recipients.

The GIS has been a mainstay for elderly women who reached age sixty-five and had never worked outside the home. That function of the GIS may be taken over by the proposed CPP homemakers' pension. Also, as many more women enter the labour force, they will earn their own CPP pensions and, it is hoped, employers' pensions.

Unlike the other pension plans, the GIS does not require that you obtain an application form yourself. Instead, as soon as your OAS application is approved, Health and Welfare Canada will automatically send you a GIS application form and a booklet explaining the details of how the plan operates. However, if you are eligible to receive benefits they will not be paid if you are out of the country for more than six months.

Many of the provinces have plans similar to the GIS which pay benefits to retired people with low incomes.

PART III

PRIVATE PENSION PLANS

5

What Kind of Plan Is It?

Education is the best provision for old age.
Aristotle

IN CONSIDERING PRIVATE, USUALLY EMPLOYER-SPONSORED; pension plans, the first question we need to answer is, "What kind of plan do you belong to?" There are two basic types of private pension plans. It is important that you understand the differences between these two types of plans and how they operate. Unfortunately, the pension industry doesn't make this easy. First, the names of the two types of plans are so similar that it is easy to confuse them. Then, to complicate matters further, one type of plan has two names that are used interchangeably.

So, what are these two types of plans? The first type is called a "defined-contribution plan" or a "money-purchase plan." The second type is a "defined-benefit plan."

A defined-contribution or money-purchase plan is like a Registered Retirement Savings Plan (RRSP). You know how much money is going into the plan but not how much you are likely to receive as a pension. In a defined-benefit plan you will have a formula to describe how much income you will receive but you won't know how much is being paid into the plan.

To illustrate the difference between them, let's consider the kind of plan that Alice belongs to and the kind that Harry belongs to. Remember, Alice works for a small manufacturing firm.

Defined-Contribution Plans

Alice's company has a pension plan under which she contributes 5 percent of her pay annually. The company matches her contribution so that, in total, a contribution of 10 percent of Alice's pay annually is made to the pension plan on her behalf. Do you see why this type of plan is called "defined-contribution"? The contributions accumulate in a separate account set up for Alice. When she retires, the full amount of the contributions plus interest will be used to purchase an annuity on her behalf. There is no risk to Alice's employer in such an arrangement. The company knows that, as long as she works there, it will be contributing 5 percent of her annual pay to the pension plan.

Right now Alice has very little idea of the amount of pension she will receive. Her pension will depend on how much she has earned each year, the rate of return on her contribution account and the rates of interest that apply when her annuity is purchased.

What is an annuity? Well, it is rather like the opposite of a mortgage. Under a mortgage you borrow a fixed sum of money and in return you pay an annual amount over so many years. Under an annuity, you pay a fixed sum of money and in return you receive payments over so many years. We all know that the annual payments under a mortgage increase when interest rates are high. In the same way, Alice will receive larger annuity payments if she buys her annuity at a time when interest rates are high.

Another common feature of a defined-contribution plan is that Alice has the option to choose different investment vehicles. She can pick a guaranteed fund, which is similar to a savings account, a common-stock fund, or a bond fund. The common-stock fund is the most risky investment for Alice because the value of her investment will go up and down as the stock market does. And you only have to read or listen to the news to know how volatile the stock market can be! At the same time, the stock market can have great potential for big gains. The bond fund is less risky than the common-stock fund but the potential income is more limited. The guaranteed fund is the safest investment but may also produce the smallest return. Alice's choice will not affect her employer's cost, therefore, she has complete freedom of choice. So which fund should she invest in? Although she only recently joined the plan, when she approaches age sixty-five, she will be dealing with a large sum of money, probably representing her major source of retirement income. Alice chose the more volatile investment fund when she joined the plan. But when she gets closer to retirement, she will likely switch to the guaranteed fund to preserve her capital.

Defined-Benefit Plans

Harry's company pension plan is different. It promises to pay him a pension based on his earnings in each year. Harry's pension will be 2 percent of his earnings during each year he was with the insurance company. This type of pension is a defined-benefit plan. Harry contributes to the fund and his employer pays in enough money to provide the benefit it is promising to pay him.

Harry knows exactly how much pension he has earned to date. Turn to page 52 for an outline of the pension he has earned until now. His employer, however, cannot calculate the extract contribution it will have to make in the future. Its contribution will be affected by the rate of return on plan investments, the length of time that employees stay with the company, and a host of other variables. In the next chapter we'll go into some of the details of how Harry's employer decides how much to contribute to the plan.

With a defined-benefit plan, it is not possible to distinguish the contributions that have been made on Harry's behalf from those made on behalf of any other employee. This situation is in direct contrast to Alice's defined-contribution plan where, you will remember, the contributions made on her behalf were kept in a separate account set up for her.

Perhaps the table on the following page will make it easier to remember the differences between the two types of plans.

To complicate matters even more, defined-benefit plans come in many different forms, based on how the pension will be calculated. The simplest type is a flat-benefit plan. Marcel, one of Harry's neighbours, belongs to this kind of plan. Marcel works as a welder

	Defined-Contribution (Money-Purchase)	Defined-Benefit
Contributions	Specified: usually a percentage of salary per year for both employee and employer.	May or may not be required from employee. If employee contribution is required, will usually be a percentage of salary. Employer's contribution is not specified and varies depending on rates of return, pension fund earnings, employee turnover, etc.
Amount of Pension	Unknown until retirement. Will depend on how much money has accumulated in employee's account and on interest rates when employee retires.	Specified: based on the number of years the employee has been with the company.
Who Selects Investments	Employee usually has a choice of several different types of accounts.	Employer chooses.
Type of Account	Individual account for each employee.	No separate employee account. All contributions go into one big pot.

for an auto-parts company and belongs to the union. Flat-benefit plans are common for unionized employees. The level of benefits that will be paid is usually increased as a result of ongoing union negotiations.

Marcel's plan is a good example of a flat-benefit plan. Marcel earns $30,000 a year and will retire from his company with a benefit of $25 a month for each year of service. He will have been with the company for twenty-five years when he retires. While Marcel is working he receives a monthly income, before tax and deductions, of $2,500. When he retires he will receive a monthly income before tax, if any, of $625 ($25 × 25 years) per month from his pension plan. His pension will replace about 25 percent of his pre-retirement income. If Marcel's earnings were $3,000 a month, he would need a pension benefit of $30 per month per year of service to provide the same level (25 percent) of income replacement.

A flat-benefit plan works best for a group of employees all of whom have similar earning levels. As well, benefit levels must be increased as the general level of earnings rises, because of inflation.

Consider Marcel's friend, Joe. He joined his pension plan in 1960 when he was forty. At that time the level of benefit was $2 per month per year of service. In 1970 the level of benefits to be earned for future service was increased to $4. In 1976 it went to $6, in 1979 to $8, in 1982 to $10, and in 1985 to $12. When Joe retired in 1985, his pension was calculated as:

10 years at $ 2	equals	$ 20	
6 years at $ 4	equals	$ 24	
3 years at $ 6	equals	$ 18	
3 years at $ 8	equals	$ 24	
3 years at $10	equals	$ 30	
		$116	

His total pension, after twenty-five years of service, was only $116 per month. Joe was a victim of the fact that the pension updates were not retroactive. If total service had been updated each time, he would have received a final pension of $300 a month ($12 × 25 years). The moral of this story is, if you are a member of this type of plan and have been with the company for a long time, make sure you are not forgotten when pension improvements are negotiated by your union or implemented by your employer.

Career-Average Plans

A different kind of defined-benefit plan is earnings related. Remember Harry? He belongs to a pension plan whereby he makes an annual contribution equal to 5 percent of his pay. The benefit he earns for each year of service is equal to 2 percent of his earnings in that year. When he retires he will receive a pension of 2 percent of his "career earnings." Expressed another way, his pension is calculated as 2 percent times his years of service times his "career-average" earnings.

Harry joined his company in 1968 when he was twenty-one. However, he wasn't eligible to join the pension plan until age twenty-six, in 1973. His earnings, contributions, and accumulated benefits have been:

Year	Earnings	Harry's Contribution (5% of earnings)	Annual Benefit Earned
1973	$ 8,000	$ 400	$ 160
1974	9,000	450	180
1975	10,000	500	200
1976	11,000	550	220
1977	13,000	650	260
1978	14,000	700	280
1979	15,000	750	300
1980	17,000	850	340
1981	20,000	1,000	400
1982	22,000	1,100	440
1983	25,000	1,250	500
1984	28,000	1,400	560
1985	30,000	1,500	600
1986	32,000	1,600	640
1987	35,000	1,750	700
1988	37,000	1,850	740
1989	39,000	1,950	780
1990	41,000	2,050	820
1991	44,000	2,200	880
			$9,000

The weakness of this type of plan from Harry's point of view is similar to the weakness of a flat-benefit plan. In a period of high inflation, the benefits earned in the past for a long-service employee become almost worthless. The solution is similar to that for a flat-benefit plan. Regular updates will keep the benefits current. Many companies update the benefits payable under their career-average plans on a regular basis, or when finances permit.

If Harry's pension is updated in 1991, to base his whole pension on 1991 earnings, he will have accumulated a pension of $16,720 (2 percent × $44,000 × 19 years) rather than the $9,000 he has accumulated now.

Final-Average Plans

This last major category of defined-benefit plans is also earnings-related, but it is designed to provide automatic updates to accumulated pensions. If Harry were in a final-average pension plan he would know that his pension would be based on his earnings near retirement. He would not be dependent on his employer making an update during the last year he works before retiring.

In a typical final-average plan, Harry's "final average" earnings would be defined as his average earnings over the five years just before retirement. For example, his final-average earnings from the previous example would be $39,200. If he retired from his company with nineteen years of service, he would be entitled to a pension of

$39,200   (final-average earnings)
×   19   (pensionable service)
×   2%   (his benefit-accrual rate)
$14,896

There are other possible definitions of final-average earnings. An average could be taken over three years, ten years, or almost any period. In rare cases it could be a final-pay plan with the whole pension based on earnings in the final year of service. The New York City Firemen's Plan illustrates the potential risk in a genuine final-pay plan. In the plan's heyday, employees who were close to retirement would furiously buy overtime from their younger colleagues in order to inflate their earnings base. As you might expect, the plan has been changed!

A common alternative is to base the pension on the "best five consecutive years of earnings in the last ten years of employment." The logic behind this alternative is that some employees experience a drop-off in their earnings as they approach retirement. By basing the pension on the best five years of earnings they are protected against a corresponding drop-off in their pension entitlement.

Of course there are hybrids of the basic types of pension plans. There are final-average plans with guaranteed money-purchase minimums. There are money-purchase plans with a final-average guarantee. A common type of arrangement in the past was a defined-benefit plan plus a money-purchase vehicle for additional voluntary contributions (AVCs).

By now you are probably wondering which type of pension plan is best. That's a difficult question to answer. The advantage of a defined-benefit plan is that you will have a pretty good idea how much pension you will receive from your employer when you retire. You can easily decide then whether you need to save more on your own. The main advantage of a defined-contribution or money-purchase plan is that you can choose how to invest your money and how much risk you are willing to take.

But all of this is really academic because you probably won't be able to choose the type of plan to belong to. Instead, your employer will have looked at the options and decided what kind of plan to put in place for employees. And, like most other things in life, pension plans go in and out of fashion. Over recent years, defined-benefit plans have been in fashion. Although they represent 40 percent of pension plans in Canada they cover 92 percent of pension-plan members. Perhaps this is the case because we have come through a time when we as a society believed that our government and our employer or our union should look after us. Now there seems to be a move to more individualism. Many people seem to want to have more choice in planning for their futures. As a result, we have seen defined-contribution (money-purchase) plans experience an increase in popularity.

Another reason defined-contribution plans have become more popular is that employers don't have to take as much risk and they know exactly how much their pension plan will cost them. On January 1, 1987, new legislation increased the costs of pension plans for employers who have defined-benefit plans. As a result, some employers are switching from defined-benefit to defined-contribution plans. Over the period from 1982 to 1988 the number of defined contribution plans doubled, while the number of defined benefit plans declined.

6

Who Pays?

While men believe in the infinite, some ponds
will be thought to be bottomless.

Henry David Thoreau

NOW THAT WE HAVE LOOKED AT the two basic kinds of pension
plans, the next question is, who pays for them?

For a money-purchase (defined-contribution) plan it is an easy
question to answer. Both the company and employee contribute
according to a preset formula. There is no risk of the employer's
being asked to increase contributions unexpectedly because the
benefit that will be paid is the amount that the accumulated contributions will buy.

For a defined-benefit plan it is more difficult to understand
how contributions are made. We have to delve into the mysterious
world of the actuary!

Now, unless your neighbour is one, or you work for an insurance company, or your son or daughter marries one, you probably
will not know what an actuary has to do with your pension plan.
Actuaries deal with statistics and probabilities. They help an
employer who sponsors a defined-benefit pension plan decide what
contribution the employer has to make to the pension plan each
year. In helping your employer, actuaries deal with the "present
value" of money.

As a starting point to understanding present values, let's suppose we want to borrow $10 from you and agree to pay it back in
ten years' time. How much should we pay you back at the end of

the ten years? Clearly, more than $10. After all, you could have earned interest on that money if you had not lent it to us. Suppose we settle on $20. You might say that the accumulated value of $10 over ten years is $20. An actuary would turn this around and say that the present value of $20 payable in ten years is $10.

Suppose we want to find the present value of a series of payments of $10 made at the beginning of each year for the next ten years? This is an annuity, payable annually in advance for ten years. It is no more difficult than finding the present value of each payment separately and adding them together.

In addition to present values, actuaries must also consider mortality, or the risk of dying. Under pension plans, benefits are not normally paid only for a fixed term such as ten years. Instead they are paid for the remaining lifetime of the plan member. Mortality tables tell the actuary the probability of an individual's being alive at a certain age. These tables are developed from studies of all the people who belong to a certain group. In the case of pension plans the group includes all people who are covered by an annuity and the table is known as a "group annuity mortality table."

Using our group annuity mortality table, and interest at 10 percent, the present value of an annuity of $10, payable annually in advance for life to an individual aged sixty-five, is calculated as follows:

Present value of first payment equals:
$10 (the first payment is being made on the date of our calculations).

Present value of second payment equals:
$10 × the present value of $1 payable one year ahead × the probability that the individual will live until age 66.

Present value of third payment equals:
$10 × the present value of $1 payable in two years' time × the probability that the individual will live until age 67.

With these basic tools the actuary can calculate the present value of a flat-dollar benefit, payable at some point in the future for the remaining lifetime of a retiring employee. The only other problem is to spread this present value over the future to establish the annual contribution needed — in actuarial jargon, the "funding" method. The ways in which the present value can be spread are infinite and are beyond the scope of this book. However, while the funding method does not affect the actual cost of the benefits, it does affect the timing of the contributions.

In a new pension plan there is normally no fund of money. The fund develops as contributions are made from year to year. One aspect of the funding method is that it looks at the present value of the benefits earned to date (the liabilities) and compares this with the value of the assets in the plan. If the value of the assets is larger than the value of the liabilities then the plan is said to be "fully funded." The amount of the assets in excess of the liability is called the "surplus." In recent years we've heard a lot about surpluses, especially in connection with Dominion Stores. We'll discuss surpluses in more detail in Chapter 19.

If the value of the assets is less than the value of the liabilities, there is said to be an "unfunded liability." In the next chapter we will see that there are rules about what a company must do if its pension plan has an unfunded liability.

The funding method also determines the annual current-service contribution or normal cost. This is the amount of the contribution that must be made during the year to keep the funding on track.

Up to this point our description of the actuary's work has been fairly simple. In reality, for a pension plan, the actuary will be concerned with much more than the rate of return to assume, the mortality table to use, and the funding method to apply. Other key considerations will include:

- the value to place on the assets;
- the probability of members of the pension plan dying, becoming disabled, or leaving the company before retirement;
- the rate of future salary increases (for a final-/best-average plan);
- the level of expenses under the plan.

The great flexibility available to actuaries is one of the reasons that their work is often so hard to understand. In addition, the jargon actuaries use makes things even more mysterious. To put it simply, the real aim of the actuary is to help determine the appropriate contribution to be made to a pension plan every year to pay the benefits promised to the members of the plan — you!

To illustrate the points we have discussed, let's look at Harry again. Suppose he wants to buy, not a pension, but a trailer at age sixty-four. He estimates that the trailer will cost him $20,000 in twenty years' time and that he can earn interest at 5 percent per year on his savings.

At age forty-four the present value of the trailer is $7,538, assuming interest at 5 percent. Let's suppose he decides to put $500 per year into a special bank account to pay for it.

At age forty-nine the present value of the trailer is $9,620. Harry figures he should have paid for a quarter of it, so he should have at least $2,405 in his bank account. He actually has $2,905 so he has a "surplus" of $500. He decides to reduce his annual savings deposit to $400.

At age fifty-four, the present value of the trailer is $12,278. He figures he should have paid for half of it, or $6,139. He only has $6,032 in his bank account, so he has an "unfunded liability" of $107. He decides to increase his annual deposit to $450.

At age fifty-nine he realizes that the cost of trailers has increased significantly. It will now probably cost him $24,000 to buy the one he wants. The present value of $24,000 payable in five years' time is $18,805. He should have paid for three-quarters of the trailer, or approximately $14,104. In fact, although he has earned 7 percent on his savings over the last five years, his bank account is only worth $11,229. He decides to increase his annual deposit to $1,000.

Over the final five years he once again earns 7 percent on his bank account. His final balance at age sixty-four is $21,902. He is able to buy the trailer on a special deal at $22,000.

This simple example demonstrates many of the features of an actuary's work: the regular reviews; the comparison of the assets accumulated against some target; the calculation of an annual-contributions requirement; the need to be flexible as circumstances change.

Back to the world of pensions! Once the required level of annual contributions has been established, the next question is the split of contributions between the employer and the employees. In some plans the employer makes all contributions. These are known as non-contributory plans. In other cases, the employee contributes a specified amount each year, usually a percentage of wage or salary, and the company contributes the rest. You will remember that Harry contributes 5 percent of his pay to his pension plan.

oH ↳ 6%

7

Who Makes the Rules?

*In general the art of government consists in
taking as much money as possible from one class
of citizens to give to the other.*

Voltaire

LIKE SO MANY OTHER THINGS that affect our lives, private pension
plans are regulated by the government. But which government?
The rules governing pension plans are complicated by Canada's
legislative structure. Under the terms of the British North America Act, pensions are a provincial responsibility.

Most company pension plans are registered with the province
in which the majority of the plan members are employed. Provincial acts were passed as follows:

Ontario	January 1, 1965
Quebec	January 1, 1966
Alberta	January 1, 1967
Saskatchewan	January 1, 1969
Manitoba	July 1, 1976
Nova Scotia	January 1, 1977
Newfoundland	January 1, 1985

In addition, a federal act was introduced on October 1, 1967. If a
company is located in a province that does not have its own act or
in the Yukon or Northwest Territories, or is federally chartered,
like a bank, then its plan is registered under the federal act.

What do the various pension acts say? In their original form most were similar and they covered many of the issues we will discuss in this book:

- benefits to be provided;
- protection if you leave the company, die, or become disabled before retiring;
- minimum funding standards;
- descriptive material to be given to employees;
- investment standards.

Generally the legislation is designed to protect you, the individual plan member. It does this three ways.

First, all pension plans have to be registered with the appropriate government. This means a document outlining the operation of the plan must be filed, also samples of the materials the company has distributed to employees to describe the plan to them and copies of the trust document or insurance contract establishing the plan.

Second, the company must file an annual information return. This includes information on membership, contributions, and any changes that have been made to the plan in the previous year.

Third, for defined-benefit plans, an actuary's certificate must be filed at least once every three years. It shows the financial position of the plan and the actuary's recommended level of contributions.

Using these three levels of information, the government involved monitors the plan and can feel fairly confident that the plan is meeting the rules.

Suppose none of these rules existed. An employer could sponsor a pension plan which might only pay benefits to the "golden-haired boys." If you were so sick you had to leave your employer before age sixty-five you might lose your total pension. The employer might never make a contribution to the plan, which would ultimately go bankrupt. You would have nowhere to turn for help.

As it is, you can always contact your provincial pension authority if you feel you are being mistreated as a member of a pension plan. A list of these agencies is provided in Appendix II.

A company is only required to register in one province even if it has plants or offices in several. However, individual employees are subject to the legislation of the province in which they work. Let's say you work in Manitoba as a salesman for a company whose head office is in Ontario. The company's pension plan would be registered in Ontario but your benefits would be paid according to Manitoba legislation. For this reason, uniformity between the various acts is desirable.

Over the last twenty years it became obvious that many of the basic elements of provincial legislation were outdated. The make-up of the workforce had changed dramatically. Employees rarely, if ever, stay in one job for their working lifetimes. We have had periods of exceptionally high inflation. And the old rules were not flexible enough to accommodate these changes. As a result, the pension system was severely criticized.

Finally, after years of meetings, task forces, commissions, and plain hard work, something close to a national consensus was achieved. New legislation was effective on January 1, 1987 — legislation that had a significant impact on every pension plan in Canada.

One underlying theme in this new legislation was that pensions were no longer merely an obligation that the employer can discharge by providing the pensions promised on the appointed dates. Instead, the popular view is that employer contributions to a pension plan are the "deferred pay" of the employee. This philosophy has had a major impact on many areas of pension-plan design and funding.

The rules in the new provincial legislation, and the logic that led to them, will be summarized in later chapters. In this chapter, we will only discuss the rules as they relate to the level of benefits that can be provided and the way these benefits can be paid for.

Basic to all the legislation is the requirement that the employer must contribute to the pension plan and must be responsible for providing the benefits as set out in the plan document. If employees contribute to the plan they must be guaranteed to receive back from the plan at least the value of their contributions plus interest, calculated on some reasonable basis.

Benefits must be uniform or accumulated in a logical fashion from year to year. This means a plan under which you earned 1 percent of final-average pay for service in 1985, $10 per month for service in 1986, 2 percent of final-average pay for service in 1987, and so on, would not be acceptable. Also, although the employer may alter the plan from time to time, benefits cannot be taken away once they have been earned.

There are a set of very complicated rules governing the way in which a company must make its contributions. In the previous chapter we described the process that an actuary goes through in preparing a "valuation" of a pension plan, determining how solvent the plan is and calculating how much the company must contribute in the current year.

If a plan has a surplus the company may be able to use the surplus to reduce its contribution for the current year. But if the plan has a deficit, the deficit must be paid off over a fixed period of years by what are called "special payments." Fifteen years is the maximum allowed to eliminate a deficit. Under certain circumstances, a province may require that a deficit be eliminated over a period as short as five years.

The government authorities make sure company contributions are being made according to the rules. They review the annual information returns and actuarial reports. In the process, they examine the assumptions the actuary has made to ensure they are reasonable.

The choice of assumptions and methods used by the actuary are not only limited by government authorities but also by the actuary's professional training and membership in the Canadian Institute of Actuaries. However, just as economists often disagree when they predict interest rates over the next year, actuaries can also have honest differences of opinion. After all they are trying to predict what could happen over a long period — from the time someone joins a plan until he dies! The job of the pension analysts at a provincial pension commission is to decide when an actuary's view of the future is too optimistic. If the actuary is too optimistic there is a risk that the employer won't contribute enough to the plan to pay the benefits he has promised his employees.

To simplify the job of the analyst, each province normally develops a range of acceptable valuation methods and assumptions. This range is not usually published, but it is well known by all actuaries.

They will only step outside the range if they feel they have strong justification.

One last point is the issue of pre-funding (another good piece of actuarial jargon!). Suppose you are an employer with a brand new plan, and that all your employees are age twenty. Logic would say that, since you will not be making any significant payments out of the plan for many years, you can wait a few years before putting any money into the plan. Not so! Provincial legislation requires that you deposit into the plan each year at least the value of the benefits being earned that year. Actually, this makes a lot of sense. After all, what would happen if ten years down the road you sold the company, or, worse still, went bankrupt? There would be no money in the plan and your employees would be left high and dry.

Bankruptcy leads us to the final requirement related to employer contributions — their security! The province of Ontario is a fairly typical example. It considers all employee contributions that an employer withholds from employees as being held in trust by the employer. Similarly, employer contributions that are due but not yet paid are considered to be held in trust by the employer and there is supposed to be a "lien and charge" on these assets for the employees. Unfortunately there are too many horror stories of companies keeping pension contributions outside the pension plan to help finance them through hard times. Once the contributions are within the plan they are safe from the demands of creditors.

Because of these problems Quebec has legislation that requires both employer and employee contributions to be deposited monthly. We'll discuss this issue further in Chapter 17, on winding up a pension plan.

Revenue Canada

The provinces are concerned with protecting the rights of the members of pension plans. Revenue Canada is also concerned with pension plans, but its concerns are quite different. Registered pension plans enjoy many attractive tax advantages. Employer and employee contributions are tax deductible within certain limits. Investment income does not attract tax. In addition a tax credit equal to the lesser of 17% of pension income or $170 is available to individuals 60 years and over and other individuals under special circumstances. Because it makes these tax concessions Revenue Canada does not want the pension system to be abused. How does it go about making sure it isn't?

In the first place, the employer has to get the pension plan registered. To prove that it is a bona fide plan, the employer must file the details of the plan, a requirement similar to that dictated by the provinces. The employer must also prove that the plan has been registered with the appropriate provincial jurisdiction. Second, the trustee files an annual return showing the details of contributions made into the plan. Third, regular actuarial reports are filed.

If a pension plan is not registered, or if it is deregistered, then none of the favourable tax treatments apply.

When Revenue Canada reviews a pension plan it wants to make sure that its requirements are being met. It will particularly check on:

- the people to be covered by the plan and the service to be recognized;
- the vehicle that has been set up to fund the benefits;
- the possibility of employees receiving a cash lump-sum payment from the plan;
- the maximum benefits to be provided on death, disability, termination, or retirement;
- the contributions to be made by the employees;
- the current-service contributions and past-service contributions to be made by the employer.

In later chapters we will look at many of these issues. Here, we are only concerned with questions about the maximum levels of benefits and the contributions that can be made.

For many years, the maximum annual contribution that an employee could make to a registered pension plan was $3,500. If the employees were not required to contribute to the plan they could still deposit up to $3,500 as additional voluntary contributions (AVCs) if the plan permitted. In some cases, if an employee had not contributed to the plan for a number of years, he or she was eligible to make additional AVCs for those years.

If the plan was a defined-contribution (money-purchase) plan, the maximum employer contribution was also $3,500 a year. This placed an automatic maximum on the level of pension an employee could receive from a money-purchase plan. It was the amount that could be bought from the accumulated contributions of $7,000 per year, payable throughout an employee's lifetime.

Let's consider an employee called Jane, currently aged thirty, in a defined-contribution pension plan. If Jane's contributions and the company's contributions were made at the maximum level every year, and earned interest at an annual rate of 8 percent, by age sixty-five Jane would have a lump sum of $1.2 million to her credit. This would be enough to buy a pension of about $120,000 a year. Sounds pretty good, you say! But let's see what inflation would have done to Jane's salary. Suppose her starting salary was $35,000 per year and she received 8 percent salary increases each year up to retirement. Her final-average salary at age sixty-five would be about $500,000, her pension would only replace 24 percent of her pre-retirement earnings ($120,000/$500,000).

If Jane had been in a defined-benefit plan under which the pension she earned for each year of service was 2 percent of her final-average earnings then you might expect that her pension at age sixty-five would be 70 percent (35 × 2 percent) of final-average earnings, or $350,000. In fact, Revenue Canada had an extra rule for defined-benefit pension plans. The pension that could be paid could not exceed 2 percent of final-average earnings, or $1,715 (whichever is less), for each year of service. In this example, Jane would have been limited to a maximum pension of $60,025.

This story points out two obvious weaknesses in the system which existed in the past. Fixed dollar maximums do not work very well in periods of inflation. The maximum pension obtainable may be bigger under a defined-benefit or a defined-contribution plan, depending on the limits applied by Revenue Canada.

To try to solve these problems, the 1985 federal budget contained proposals to overhaul the tax system as applied to pension plans. The whole thing was very complex, but there were three critical recommendations:

1. The annual maximum contribution by the employer and the employee combined should be 18 percent of the employee's pay.
2. The $1722 maximum pension limit per year of service for defined-benefit plans would be indexed to the average Industrial Wage after 1990.
3. The maximum contribution to a defined-contribution plan would be increased in stages to $15,500 in 1990 and would be indexed after that.

In practice these rules have been delayed again and again; however, at the time of writing it is expected that they will finally be introduced by January 1, 1991. Because of the delays, the year in which the system will be mature and indexing will begin is now 1995 rather than 1990. The logic underlying the approach is based on the theory that, taking the average pension plan member, a pension of $2 has an equivalent value to the contribution of $18. If we accept this relationship then we will agree that an 18% contribution to a defined contribution vehicle is equivalent in value to a 2% final average pension. We would also accept that, for a lucky individual earning $86,111, his maximum annual contribution will be $15,500 (18% of $86,111) and that his maximum pension per year of service will be $1,722 (2% of $86,111).

It certainly is possible to justify the "9 times rule" as an average, if we anticipate that all defined benefits will be indexed in retirement and that the pension will continue to be paid to the surviving spouse at 60% of the original value following the death of the pensioner. Like all averages, however, this factor discriminates by age. A sixty-year-old could never purchase a $2 indexed pension for $18. A twenty-year-old could buy many times that amount thanks to the "magic of compound interest".

The new rules will be relatively easy to administer for an individual who is wholly committed to a defined contribution or defined benefit approach. For those of us who wish to be in both types of plans, the government has invented the "Pension Adjustment". Let's look at the example of Jane, who earns $35,000 in 1990 and belongs to a 2% defined benefit plan. Her Pension Adjustment for 1990 will be nine times the pension she earned in

1990 less $1,000. This adjustment will be deducted from her eligible RRSP contributions for 1991. In the example given, Jane's Pension Adjustment for 1990 will be ($35,000 × two percent × nine) less $1,000 or $5,300. The critical question: does Jane value the pension she has earned in 1990 as highly as a potential RRSP contribution of $5,300 in 1991.

The new tax rules are complex. However, it is clear that the rules have the power to influence pension plan design. Already, employees are asking to be released from defined benefit pension plans so that they can maximize their future RRSP contributions. In addition, the 9 times rule is totally unselective. It applies equally to the young and old; final average, career average and flat benefit plans; and indexed and non-indexed benefits.

Different plans will provide different value for money and this will impact directly on your ability to save for retirement through an RRSP. Many employers will redesign their pension plans to obtain maximum tax advantages for themselves and their employees.

One other twist is the Past Service Pension Adjustment (PSPA). You might think that a way of avoiding the PAs was to provide low levels of defined benefits now and to improve the plan at some point in the future. You would be wrong! The government will go back and calculate what PAs you should have had if the amendment had been in effect since 1990, then you'll be hit with a retroactive adjustment to your RRSP room. Clever aren't they!

You will remember that when the provincial authorities review a pension-plan valuation, they want to make sure that the actuary has not been too optimistic in his or her projections and to be sure that the employee's rights have been protected. A Revenue Canada analyst reviews a valuation report to be sure that the actuary has not been too pessimistic. He or she will question the report if it seems to make an unnecessarily large provision for accrued benefits or if it appears to anticipate pension payments over and above the maximum. To some extent, when actuaries prepare their reports they try to steer a course between a line of provincial analysts shouting "not too little" and a line of Revenue Canada analysts shouting "not too much."

In addition, if the actuary's report shows an unfunded liability, or deficit, then the employer must write and request approval for the special payments. This prevents employers from manipulating the results each year to obtain the most favourable tax position.

As a final precaution, Revenue Canada requires that, if a valuation reveals a surplus of more than two years' company current-service contributions, company contributions to the plan must stop until the surplus is reduced. The logic here is to prevent a plan from "salting away" contributions that it does not really need.

Who Else Makes the Rules?

In addition to the specific rules that govern pension plans, most other legislation has some effect on pensions.

Human rights legislation, particularly the Charter of Rights, addresses discrimination on the basis of age, sex, or marital status. Family law has an impact on the rights of employees and their beneficiaries. Trust law limits the powers of pension-plan trustees, the people who look after the money. Insurance law stipulates the types of investments a pension plan can participate in. Industrial relations law, governing work stoppages and lay-offs, dictates what happens to pension plan benefits and contributions.

You may be wondering why, with all these rules, the private pension plan system seems to have so many problems. In fact, the private pension plan system could be a great deal worse. Canada is lucky that comprehensive pension legislation was introduced in the mid-1960s, before the situation got out of hand. However, when the original acts were drafted in the 1960s, they did not anticipate the problems of the 1980s. After twenty years the system needed to be brought up to date. The pressures brought on by the severe recession in the early 1980s caused many employers to exploit the flexibility of the system. Updated rules should help to clarify just how far they can go.

The main weakness of the private pension system is that there is nothing in any of the rules that forces an employer to have a pension plan or to provide a minimum level of benefits or to have inflation protection.

8

Am I Eligible?

*Youth is the time of getting, middle age of
improving and old age of spending; a negligent
youth is usually attended by an ignorant middle
age, and both by an empty old age.*

Anne Bradstreet

ONE OF THE REASONS HARRY AND ALICE have become so concerned
about planning for their retirement years is because of something
that happened to their friend Ingrid.

Ingrid works with Harry at the insurance company. She was
twenty when she joined the company. At that time, males were
eligible to join the pension plan at age twenty-five, and females at
age thirty. Ingrid didn't really mind. At age twenty she wasn't interested in pensions.

Ten years later, when she was eligible to join, she discovered
that employees had to contribute 5 percent of pay annually. She
and her husband had just bought a larger house and were saving
to buy new furniture. Ingrid decided to delay joining for a few
years. At age forty, she considered joining the plan again and discussed it with her husband. He was already enrolled in his employer's pension plan and they knew they would both receive Old
Age Security and Canada Pension Plan benefits. They decided they
would have enough to meet their retirement needs without Ingrid
joining her company plan.

Recently, Ingrid's husband died and she received a refund of
the contributions he made to his pension plan with interest. Ingrid,

now age fifty, has joined her company's pension plan. She realizes that the final pension she will receive will be inadequate and so does her employer. Ingrid feels the system has failed her. Has it?

Participation in Ingrid's and Harry's pension plan is voluntary. The opposite of voluntary participation is compulsory participation. Compulsory participation is usually acceptable to employees if they are not required to contribute anything to the pension plan. The problem in Canada is that we have a tradition of requiring employees to contribute to private pension plans. Because of this, many employers have been reluctant to make plan membership compulsory. They are afraid of upsetting good employees who, for whatever reason, do not want to contribute to the plan. As well, there are many contributory plans in Canada in which fewer than 50 percent of the eligible employees participate. The employer knows that, in the future, it will see long-term employees retire with no company pension, a situation that undermines one of the traditional reasons for having a pension plan — as a reward for long service.

The usual solution to this problem was to set up a "recruitment drive" and try to sign up new members. These drives were not usually very successful. First, if a plan had a low rate of participation for a number of years, the negative attitude towards it was hard to overcome. Second, there was the possibility that a large number of older employees would respond to the drive, a situation which substantially increased the employer's contributions. Enough to make the employer think twice!

There are better solutions to the problem of voluntary participation. Some employers have replaced the contributory plan with a combination of a non-contributory basic plan and a voluntary group Registered Retirement Savings Plan. Others have introduced a two-tier system under which employees who contribute receive a higher benefit than those who do not contribute. Still others have introduced two-tier eligibility conditions. Membership is optional for younger employees and compulsory for employees at a certain age — often thirty. This approach provides some flexibility for individuals to make their own decisions.

The issue of mandatory participation in private pension plans has not really been resolved. The majority opinion is still that Canadians should be given a choice whether or not to join company pension plans.

The consensus that emerged from the pension reform process is that "every employee of a class of employees for whom a pension plan is established must be eligible to be a member of the plan." For example, if you are a salaried employee working for a company that has a salaried employees' pension plan, you must be eligible to join the plan. The plan may provide for a waiting period of up to twenty-four months (under federal or Ontario law), two calendar years (under Alberta rules) or one calendar year (under Quebec rules).

Probably your next question is, why have eligibility requirements at all? If employees don't have to contribute, why not bring all of them in on their first day of employment? To answer this question we must remember the original reason that pension plans were established. For many employers it was a way of rewarding long-service employees. Statistics show that employee turnover is highest among young, short-service employees. Obviously, then, an employer saves a great deal of administrative work by excluding young employees from the plan. In addition, remember the Revenue Canada limits we discussed in Chapter 7. In a 2 percent final-average pension plan the maximum number of years of pensionable service is thirty-five. Therefore, if twenty-year-olds were allowed into such a plan they would reach their maximum service by age fifty-five. What would the employer do with them then?

Another historical feature of eligibility conditions affected Ingrid. Traditionally women were eligible to join plans later than men. No one expected them to stay with the company — the assumption, based on stereotype, was that they would leave the company to start a family. Experience and human rights legislation have done away with this approach.

At the other end of the age scale, employees hired above a certain age, such as fifty-five, were also traditionally excluded. Although these employees often had the greatest need, they were not admitted into the pension plan because it would have been uneconomic. Human rights legislation is also eliminating this practice.

The third group generally excluded from pension plans was

part-time employees. The traditional view was that these employees did not want to divert any portion of their pay toward pension benefits. While this argument may have some validity, it must be weighed against the needs of the large number of single parents who are able to work only part time.

The new pension legislation addresses the problem of part-time employees. If they are part of a class of employees who have a pension plan, they must be eligible to join. However, in most provinces, they must have earned at least 35 percent of the C/QPP Year's Maximum Pensionable Earnings in two consecutive calendar years. For example, an hourly paid part-time employee who earned at least $8,190 (35 percent of $23,400) in 1985 and at least $9,030 (35 percent of $25,800) in 1986 would have been eligible to join an established pension plan for hourly paid employees on January 1, 1987. In Ontario part-time employees can also become eligible by working 700 hours in two consecutive years. In Quebec the rule requires 700 hours in one calendar year.

This legislation should have a major impact on organizations that have non-contributory pension plans and on the large number of part-time employees who have previously been excluded. The question is, will some employers keep earnings for part-timers below 35 percent of the YMPE? This happened when similar legislation was passed in the United States.

What happens if you are a part-time employee who earns enough to be admitted to a pension plan but your earnings fall below the 35 percent threshold figure? Do you automatically leave the plan again? No, once you are in the plan, you can stay. Similarly, if you go from full-time to part-time status you can stay in the plan.

A final point to consider is the possibility that the design of the standard pension plan may make it unsuitable for part-time employees. In that case, the legislation allows the employer to set up a second, equivalent plan for part-timers.

If you are a part-time employee who is offered membership in a contributory pension plan, what should you do? In theory you should compare the importance to you of giving up some current take-home pay in order to increase your retirement income. If you can't make up your mind, try to figure out just how much the employer will be contributing for you. Chapter 22 will help you.

As might be expected, Revenue Canada is much more explicit in its definition of employees who are *not* eligible to join pension plans. The plan must be for the sole benefit of employees, their beneficiaries, or their estates. It is not possible to add a few extra individuals to make up the numbers! In addition, there are specific rules limiting the participation of significant shareholders, self-employed individuals, partners, and proprietors. We'll spare you the details!

Revenue Canada also limits the service that may be credited under a pension plan. In essence, they want to be sure that any service that is credited will create taxable income for the employer. As a result they will include as service such things as short periods of service outside Canada, paid leaves, periods of disability, maternity leaves, and active service in the Canadian armed forces.

Including periods of disability is an important item that will be discussed in Chapter 11 on disability benefits. Including maternity leave is a controversial practice, but is secondary to the question of receiving pay for maternity leave. Under the wording of most pension plans, if pay is received for maternity leave, then it is treated as credited service. Naturally, if employees have to contribute to the pension plan the contributions would be withheld from the pay received during maternity leave.

Next, there is the question of when eligibility conditions might be waived. Consider three major situations.

First, if a company is trying to recruit a senior employee, it normally has the power to waive any waiting period and bring the employee into the plan. Second, if your company transfers you from one country to another or from one category of employee to another (e.g., from hourly paid to salaried), any service you have previously had with the employer should be used toward satisfying the eligiblity rules. For example, if there is a two-year waiting period to join the salaried pension plan, but you have already worked for four years as an hourly paid employee, you should be brought straight into the salaried plan. Under these circumstances, always make sure that you know what is going to happen to your previously accrued pension. Third, if the company you work for is acquired by another company, similar considerations apply: your prior service must be recognized under the terms of the new pension plan. Make sure you know what is happening to your original pension.

No chapter on eligibility would be complete without a discussion of another magic word, "coverage." One of the major weaknesses of the private-pension system is that only a small number of employees are actually covered by private pension plans.

In the Government of Canada publication *Better Pensions for Canadians*, the percentages of private-sector employees who are covered by a pension plan were shown to be:

Earnings	Males % Covered	Females % Covered
0 - 7,500	51.1	20.5
7,500 - 15,000	43.5	38.5
15,000 - 22,500	55.9	62.3
over 22,500	70.2	71.0
all	55.5	33.3

This table was based on 1979 statistics. A pension plan was taken to be either a private plan or an RRSP.

The findings are shocking and also hard to believe. We know there are employees who have decided not to join pension plans, employees who are ineligible, and employees who work for small companies with no pension plans. But how can the numbers of employees covered be this low?

In September 1983 the Business Committee on Pension Policy (BCPP) analysed the government statistics further. It concluded:

54 percent of full-time employed paid workers were covered under employment pension plans in 1980; persons not covered are primarily:
- low-income workers;
- employees under the age of 25;
- part-time workers;
- employees of small employers.

For many of these workers, membership in employment plans may not be desirable or necessary. For example, for persons under the age of 25 saving for retirement is not a high priority. Small employers may be financially unable to undertake the cost of a pension plan. In many cases, the small employer will provide other forms of savings such as a deferred profit sharing plan or ownership in the company.

The situation has changed little in the last ten years. Mandatory coverage by private pension plans is one of the options available to help solve the problem. Millions of people would be affected by such a change. The obvious risk is that it could provide pensions to people when they do not necessarily need them, at the expense of the future profitability of many small employers and marginal industries.

9

Do I Have to Wear a Three-Piece Suit to be Vested?

As for a future life, every man must judge for himself between conflicting probabilities.

Charles Darwin

ANOTHER REASON HARRY AND ALICE QUESTION the probability that they'll have enough to live on when they retire, is because they have seen what happened to Tony, their next-door neighbour. He has just retired. Except for his Old Age Security and CPP benefits, he has only a small pension from his employer. What happened? To find out, we need to look at Tony's work history.

He was hired by his first company at age eighteen. He joined the contributory pension plan at age twenty-one. But when he was age forty-four he left the company after twenty-six years' service. At that time, he received a refund of his contributions to the pension plan plus interest at 3 percent. He needed a new car at the time so promptly spent the full amount of his refund. Tony's new company had a non-contributory pension plan. When he left nine years later, at age fifty-three, he got nothing from the plan. He stayed with his third employer until he reached age sixty-five. His pension is based only on his last twelve years of work.

Tony thinks the private pension system has failed him. He belonged to pension plans for forty-four years. He had a fairly stable work history. But his pension was too small.

Tony's story is really about vesting. As we have said, there are two major types of private pension plans: defined-contribution (money-purchase) plans and defined-benefit plans. Under both types of plans you may or may not have to contribute. Under the defined-contribution type, your employer's contribution will be based on a formula, usually a percentage of your pay. Under the defined-benefit type, your employer's contribution will be based on an actuary's recommendation of how much is required to provide the benefits promised to you and other employees. Strictly speaking, vesting refers to the point at which, if you leave the company, you are entitled to a pension payable at some point in the future. It is usually taken to be the point at which you are entitled to some of the money paid into the plan on your behalf by your employer.

Under historic provincial and federal legislation you were vested when you reached age forty-five and completed ten years of service with the company (commonly known as "forty-five and ten"). Tony lost out on any company money because he was not yet forty-five when he left his first employer. All he got back were his own contributions plus interest. He lost out at his second employer because he left with less than ten years of service.

You probably think Tony was crazy to work for two employers for so long and then leave just before he was vested. Maybe he was ill-informed. Maybe he chose deliberately to leave his first employer at that time. Maybe his second employer encouraged him to leave. We will explore these possibilities later.

Many different types of vesting rules have been used by companies in the past:

- age and service — such as "forty-five and ten";
- service only — such as Manitoba's five-year vesting;
- age plus service — such as Saskatchewan's rule that age and service must total forty-five;
- sliding scale — unlike the other formulae where you are either vested or not (so-called "cliff-vesting"), under this formula you are vested in a percentage of your employer's contributions. The percentage increases in line with service. For example:

Vested Percentage	Service
50%	5 years
60%	6 years
70%	7 years
80%	8 years
90%	9 years
100%	10 years

Over the past twenty years the trend has been to more liberal vesting. The table below shows the vesting formulae used on the basis of information provided by Statistics Canada in the publication *Pension Plans in Canada 1988*.

	Plans		Members	
	No.	%	No.	%
Immediate Vesting	7,735	36.4	314,949	6.5
10 years or less of service or participation	3,355	15.8	1,725,354	35.6
11-19 years of service or participation	265	1.2	39,966	0.8
20 or more years of service or participation	181	0.9	28,046	0.6
Service or participation and/or age	150	0.7	42,442	0.9
Other	295	1.4	272,467	5.6
Minimum provincial standards	9,258	43.6	2,421,883	50.0
Total	21,239	100.0	4,845,107	100.0

Why did pension plans start out with such poor vesting? Again, let's remember some of the original reasons that companies introduced pension plans. One of the obvious incentives was that a company pension plan would provide you with a strong reason to stay with your employer rather than move to a competitor. Training you cost money and there was a certain appeal to providing "golden hand-cuffs."

Unfortunately, this type of logic, if taken too far, can put great pressure on you. Suppose you were in a pension plan with no vesting whatsoever: if you stayed until age sixty-five you got a full pension; if you left beforehand you got nothing. If you were aged sixty, then whatever your state of health or natural inclination, you would desperately try to stay in the job until age sixty-five. Such a situation puts a great deal of power in the hands of your employer.

It is with this in mind that the major pension-benefits acts of the 1960s were drafted with the "forty-five and ten" rule. It was seen as a compromise between you and your employer. Your employer wanted a few roadblocks in your path in case you were thinking of leaving. But now you knew your pension was protected once you met the minimum standards.

Why is there a trend towards improving vesting standards? Over the last few decades there has been a change in work patterns. At one time it was common for an employee to work all his or her life for one employer. However, today that is rare. Economists tell us that mobility of labour is a good thing in a free-market economy. Therefore, employers should remove all barriers to easy transition from one company to another. In this environment shorter vesting periods are desirable.

While these economic changes have been taking place, there has been increasing public acceptance of the view that pensions are "deferred pay." This is a complicated issue. However, the basic argument is that company contributions made on your behalf are really your money as soon as they are paid into the pension plan. If you accept this concept, then it is only logical to anticipate immediate vesting of all employer contributions.

It is not surprising that the consensus in the discussions on changing the pension system was for much shorter minimum vesting periods. The most common is for vesting based on two years of plan membership.

These rules apply only to benefits earned after January 1, 1987. Harry was hired in 1968, joined the pension plan in 1973, and is now aged forty-four. What if he decides to leave the company on January 1, 1992? Previously his pension plan granted vesting at "forty-five and ten" so he would not be eligible for any company contributions made on his behalf before January 1, 1987. However, he would be eligible for company contributions made on his behalf for the five years, 1987 through 1991.

Does this represent a major improvement in Harry's position? Consider:

1. Many companies have voluntarily introduced vesting schedules which are more generous than "forty-five and ten." In addition, some provinces, notably Manitoba and Saskatchewan, had previously introduced more liberal vesting rules.
2. If the two-year vesting had been made retroactive, many employers would have complained of the cost. They would have argued that, if they had known about two-year vesting, they would not have provided such generous benefits.

Whether or not we accept these arguments, the solution is not ideal. Employers are effectively administering two different pension plans, one for pre-1987 and one for post-1987 benefits. Existing employees may continue to be haunted by "forty-five and ten" vesting for many years to come. For example, if you are currently aged thirty, it could be fifteen years before you are finally vested for the work you did before January 1, 1987.

What Is Locking-in?

Coupled with vesting is the concept of "locking-in." Locking in basically means you cannot "pass GO and collect $200." If you leave a company and are entitled to company pension contributions, you will not be given a cheque for these contributions. Instead you will have to wait until you are sixty-five. Then you will receive monthly pension cheques from your employer. The logic here is that, had you remained with the company until retirement, you would only have benefited from your employer's pension contribution at that time. Why should you benefit earlier because you are leaving? The company contributions will be "locked in" and paid to you in some form at retirement. If you made compulsory contributions to the plan they will be "locked in" also.

Earlier in this chapter we suggested that Tony might have deliberately left his job at age forty-four. Now do you see why? Suppose his own contributions with interest totalled $15,000. If he waited another year he would be vested, his contributions would be "locked in," and he could not use them until age sixty-five. By leaving when he did he gave himself a cash windfall. This looks like a good example of short-term gain for long-term pain!

Historically, the benefit paid to a vested employee who left the company was described as a "deferred pension." Since you were entitled to the company contribution made on your behalf, it seemed reasonable to say that you had earned the full pension for service up until the date you left. You had only to wait until you reached the normal retirement date under this plan and pension payments would begin.

Unfortunately the flaw in this argument is provided by our old nemesis, inflation. When there was no inflation, the system worked well. If you were vested in three pension plans, representing different periods of your work history, you could expect to receive three pension cheques a month. In total, these cheques would be equivalent to the amount you would have received if you had stayed with one employer throughout your career.

In inflationary times, however, there is normally a mechanism built into any private plan that protects its active members from the worst aspects of inflation. In a final-average type plan that mechanism is the fact that pensions are based on pay near retirement. In a flat-dollar or career-average plan, updates are usually granted at regular intervals.

For a deferred pensioner (someone who left the company with a locked-in pension), no such mechanism exists. The pension entitlement calculated on the date of termination is normally frozen until retirement age.

Had he stayed with his first employer until age forty-five and become vested, Tony would probably have found that, by age sixty-five the value of his pension would have been so badly eroded by inflation that it was worthless. Perhaps, after all, it was a good idea to buy the car!

One solution to this problem would be to require that all deferred pensions be increased on a regular basis in line with some index based on the cost of living or the Average Industrial Wage. This approach would certainly solve your problem. The question is, who would pay for the cost of this indexing?

If we ask your original employer, the answer will be that since you are no longer contributing to the profitability of the company, your original employer should not be liable for any additional costs. Later employers will, of course, argue that it cannot be their responsibility since you were not employed by them for the years in question.

Another solution is contained in the word "portability." If the value of your deferred vested pension was calculated when you terminated, then this value could be transferred into your next employer's pension plan and used to "purchase" service time equivalent to the years accrued in the previous plan. This approach would work if both plans had the same actuarial assumptions and methods and the same benefit formula. Unfortunately, most often it is impossible to agree on the amount of the assets to be transferred.

At this point we have to consider an actuarial matter briefly. In a previous chapter we said that, the younger you are, the less it costs to buy a unit of pension. As a result, if you are a young, vested employee leaving a contributory plan, it is quite possible that your contributions alone are enough to pay for the pension you have earned. This actuarial consideration gives rise to a vicious triangle. How is it possible to encourage shorter vesting, when this may only involve locking in your money, with no matching company contribution?

This problem was first addressed by Saskatchewan in 1981, where legislation was introduced that made two important breakthroughs. It established a standard basis for calculating the value of a deferred pension and it required that the employer pay for at least half of the pension. The basis used to establish the value was open to some question since it did not allow for the future effects of inflation. Using this basis made it extremely likely that employee contributions alone would be sufficient to pay for the pension.

The new legislation attempts to settle these issues in two ways. First, if you leave a pension plan and are entitled to a vested pension, your employer must give you the option of transferring the present value of the pension you have earned, often referred to as the "commuted value." This value may be rolled into a Registered Retirement Savings Plan or into another pension plan, or it may be used to buy an annuity. In any event, you cannot take the cash. The value must ultimately be used to buy a life annuity payable not more than ten years before normal retirement age.

Second, at least 50 percent of any vested pension must be provided from employer contributions. Suppose you leave your employer and are entitled to a vested pension which has a value of $2,000 and your contributions with interest total $1,500. Your employer would have to pay at least $1,000 toward the cost of your pension.

If the system described above had been in place while Tony was working, he would have established a locked-in RRSP account at age forty-four when he would have received a lump-sum payment from his first employer's pension plan. This lump sum would have included his contributions with interest. At age fifty-three he would have put in an additional payment from his second employer. At sixty-five he would have used the balance in his RRSP account to buy an annuity which would have provided supplemental income to the pension he received from his third employer.

10

When Will I Retire?

*For solitude sometimes is best society and short
retirement urges sweet return.*

John Milton

RECENTLY HARRY GOT ANOTHER INTRODUCTION into the world
of actuarial science. Barbara, one of his claims approvers, decided
that she wanted to retire before age sixty-five. Barbara had joined
the company pension plan when she joined the company, at age
thirty-five. Now, twenty years later, she has decided to retire. She
knows that the pension plan allows early retirement as long as she
is at least fifty-five and has been with the company for ten years.
Her latest pension statement showed that she has already earned a
pension of $1,000 a month. She thinks that she can survive on this
amount plus her savings. The other day she told the personnel manager that she planned to retire. She was shocked to find that her
actual pension would only be $500 a month. What had happened
to the other $500?

There are two main reasons why Barbara's pension was reduced
so drastically. One reason has to do with mortality; the other with
compound interest.

First, let's look at mortality. The average sixty-five-year-old
woman can expect to live for approximately twenty years, or to
age eighty-five. By the same token, a fifty-five-year-old will probably live for thirty years. By retiring at fifty-five, Barbara is increasing the period of time over which her pension will likely be paid by
50 percent, from twenty years to thirty years.

Someone has to pay for all these pension benefits. The company won't voluntarily agree to increase its costs by 50 percent. The alternative is to decrease the amount of the pension it pays to Barbara.

The second major reason for the reduction is our old friend compound interest. In Chapter 6 we described how a company sets its contribution level. The contributions it makes, plus interest, will be enough to provide the benefits promised. In Barbara's case the company arranged to provide benefits to her at age sixty-five. If Barbara retires ten years early then the company has lost ten years of interest on its contributions. This, too, explains the reduction in her pension.

Let's take a look at Barbara's pension statement again. It showed that she had already earned a pension of $1,000 a month. If she had read the small print, she would have noticed that she has earned a pension of $1,000 a month payable at age sixty-five. It probably also points out that if she retires at age fifty-five there will be an early-retirement reduction.

Barbara's example demonstrates the need for every pension plan to define a normal retirement age — that is, the age at which the standard formula pension will be paid. In most cases the normal retirement age is sixty-five, although there are cases where it is sixty-two, sixty, or even younger.

Defined-Benefit Plans

Most defined-benefit plans also permit early retirement as long as certain age and service requirements are met. As was the case for Barbara and Harry, age fifty-five with ten years of service is the most common formula.

In designing a defined-benefit pension plan, the table of early-retirement reduction factors is one of the features an employer must choose. As we said earlier, these factors give a reduction of approximately 50 percent for someone retiring ten years early. The actual reduction that will be used depends on the rates of interest and the mortality table used by the actuary in calculating the factors.

Today many companies use a simpler formula (for example, three-tenths of 1 percent per month) rather than the pure actuarial reduction factor. In essence, the employer subsidizes employees who retire early. Why? There are a number of reasons.

- In a "final-average" type pension plan the employee who retires early gives up the right to have his pension based on earnings near age sixty-five. Many employers feel that the combination of the reduced earnings base and the full actuarial reduction is too great a penalty.
- In some situations, employers *want* to encourage employees to retire earlier than the normal retirement age. They use the early-retirement reduction factors as a tool to help them.
- Early retirement has been an issue in many union negotiations recently. Often the level of the reduction factors is included in the collective-bargaining agreement.

Special Early Retirement

The next step up from subsidizing early retirement by using simpler factors is to forgo using an early retirement factor. Such "special" early retirement normally also depends on age and service conditions. They are usually more stringent than the "fifty-five and ten" rule we discussed before. These are some typical conditions:

- thirty years of service regardless of age (the classic "thirty and out" pioneered by the United Auto Workers);
- thirty years of service and age sixty;
- age plus service total at least eighty-five (eighty-five points).

Now back to Barbara's case. Clearly, if a company allows all of its employees to retire at age fifty-five with an unreduced pension, it could be doubling the cost of its pension plan. In addition, if the company operates in an industry in which experience is important, it may be acting against its own best interests if it encourages key employees to retire early.

Usually the cost of an early-retirement feature is greatly reduced because many employees don't want to retire early. Even with an unreduced pension, they may be concerned that future rates of inflation will make their pension income inadequate. By continuing to work and remaining active members of the pension plan, they can earn additional pension for each year of service.

Open-Window Policies

Last on our list of early-retirement practices is the "open-window" policy. Many organizations used this approach during the 1982-83 recession when they wanted to reduce their workforces. Because of the seniority policies of unions, companies have traditionally let younger, shorter-service employees go first during a lay-off. As lay-offs spread into white-collar staffs, employers began to realize this "last in, first out" policy could undermine the future of the company. These organizations felt it would be better for their future growth in a post-recession period if they made their cutbacks from among older employees. They tried to achieve this by offering a special early-retirement package for a limited period of time. These packages included a number of special features:

- "special early retirement" with no reduction;
- crediting of additional periods of service which would have been worked between the early-retirement age and the normal-retirement age;
- paying a "bridging" benefit from the early-retirement age to age sixty-five. (We will talk more about bridging benefits in a moment.)

Many of these open-window policies were very successful in meeting company objectives. However, some were too successful. They rebounded on the employer because some of the employees who took the packages were confident that they could get a job somewhere else. Often these were the people management would have liked to keep. Conversely, the employees who rejected the offer were those people who wouldn't have been able to get a job anywhere else.

Bridging Benefits

In the previous section we referred to "bridging" benefits — another feature of early-retirement programs. They arise from the fact that, before January 1, 1987, both Canada Pension Plan and Old Age Security benefits were only paid from age sixty-five or later. Therefore, an employee who retired at age sixty with a pension of $1,200 a month would have his or her income rise to around $1,800 a month when he or she reached age sixty-five and started to receive government pensions.

If a company wanted to make early retirement look more attractive, it would pay an extra "bridging" benefit from the early-retirement date until age sixty-five. Frequently these benefits were negotiated through collective bargaining. They are not nearly as expensive to provide as regular benefits, because they are paid only for a short period. Therefore, they were an ideal sweetener for an early-retirement program.

On January 1, 1984, the Quebec Pension Plan was amended to pay a reduced pension from age sixty. This amendment has now been extended to the Canada Pension Plan. As a result, there will likely be a decline in the use of bridging.

Postponed Retirement

Just as there are reductions for employees who retire early, there are increase factors for employees who retire after their normal retirement age. The same logic applies: a seventy-year-old can expect to live five years less than a sixty-five-year-old; assets which were being accumulated to age sixty-five will earn an extra five years' interest by age seventy.

While many plans do provide post-retirement increases, the practice is not universal, for several reasons:

- In the first place, the company makes a profit under the pension plan if an employee retires late and does not receive an increased pension — a powerful incentive to do nothing.
- In Chapter 6, on contributions, we saw that the older an employee is, the more it costs to buy his or her annual pension entitlement. Many employers feel that, if they allow their employees to continue to earn pensions after age sixty-five then that is costing them quite enough.
- Just as some employers want to discourage valuable employees from retiring early, many also want to encourage non-productive employees to retire at their normal retirement age.

What if you are an employee over sixty-five whose employer does not provide for actuarial increases after normal retirement age? Revenue Canada allows you to receive a pension and keep working. Go for it!

Money-Purchase Plans

The features we have discussed so far in this chapter apply only to defined-benefit plans. Defined-contribution plans (money-purchase plans) are much easier to understand. Remember, under a defined-contribution plan, your contributions accumulate in your account until you retire and buy an annuity. If you retire early, the amount of money in your account will be smaller and the monthly payment from your annuity will be lower. If you retire late, your account will be larger and will buy a larger monthly payment from your annuity.

Discrimination

Retirement age has been one of the major areas of discussion in the debate about pensions. Much of the debate pertains to the question of discrimination.

Early in the history of pension plans the issue concerned discrimination by sex. In Britain it was traditional to allow normal retirement at age sixty-five for males, at age sixty for females. While superficially this may seem very gallant, it is illogical. After all, women usually outlive men. In any event, this practice does discriminate by sex. By now, any Canadian plan that includes this provision should have been amended.

The second area of discussion is that of early retirement. At one time it was common to have two sets of early-retirement reduction factors. One set would cover early retirement at the request of the employee. The other, more favourable set would cover early retirement at the request of the employer. Current human rights legislation generally does not allow a company to force an employee to retire before age sixty-five. Plans in which this type of provision existed have been amended to refer to "early retirement at the request of the employer with the consent of the employee."

By far, the most contentious discrimination issue is that of "mandatory retirement" at age sixty-five. For employers the idea of a mandatory-retirement age is rooted in the belief that older workers are not as efficient as younger ones, and yet salaries generally continue to increase the longer an employee is with the company. Thus, a long-term employee eventually reaches the point at which the value of his or her service is less than his or her salary or wages.

A mandatory-retirement age gives employers a clear standard they can apply to everyone. A spokesman for the Canadian Manufacturers' Association commented, "If you know that someone who is sixty-two is going to retire at sixty-five, you can let him coast a little." According to this spokesman, "this practice would be threatened if there was no guarantee that the person would be retired within a few years." A spokesman for the Business Council on National Issues added that criteria other than age, such as competence, "are a lot more nebulous and messy to get a handle on."

The employer's position has supporters in the academic community Blossom Wigdor, a psychology professor at the University of Toronto and chair-person for the National Advisory Council on Aging, says at some point people are no longer competent in their jobs. Her colleague Morley Gunderson, a professor of economics and industrial relations, adds that eliminating mandatory-retirement age could cause as many problems for older workers as it cures. He believes banning mandatory retirement would lead to more older workers being dismissed, "new competence tests, termination systems and pressure from colleagues to leave may be harder on people than the adjustment to compulsory retirement at a certain age."

Despite their focus on job security and seniority for older workers, unions agree with employers on the need for a mandatory-retirement age. For unions, mandatory retirement is a way of passing work on from one generation to another. Their support for mandatory retirement is also based on the fact that unionized workers are often in physically demanding or tedious jobs with little job satisfaction. When Cliff Pilkey was president of the Ontario Federation of Labour he was quoted as saying, "We don't want to die with our boots on. Working until you die is an archaic idea from the eighteenth century. Surely by the time anyone is sixty-five they've made their contribution to society."

On the other side of the argument, those against mandatory retirement contend that age sixty-five was established when life expectancies were much lower. Moreover, those who are living longer are generally healthier than their forebears as a result of improved health care and advances in the treatment of such conditions as heart disease and cancer.

There is also a financial argument against forcing people to retire at age sixty-five. Although some people can retire quite comfortably at age sixty-five, many people face the prospect of a lower standard of living, if not poverty, if they must stop working at that age. A 1984 study by the National Council of Welfare blamed this on the fact that most working Canadians are not covered by employer-sponsored pension plans. In a 1990 study, the council argued for retirement at age 60 without penalty under the C/QPP to help prepare for the population boom of senior citizens early in the 21st century. The council argued that this makes sense, given the problems of older workers in finding jobs. "The plain truth is that make-work jobs are the best many workers nearing retirement can hope for."

The main argument against mandatory retirement at a specific age is the injustice in forcing capable people to retire.

Certainly, employers who offer early-retirement programs admit they lose some valuable people. An all-party parliamentary committee, which reviewed all federal statutes and laws in terms of Section 15 of the Charter of Rights, argued along this line in urging an end to mandatory retirement. A report in the October 16, 1985, issue of the *Toronto Star* quoted from the committee's report:

> Mandatory retirement does not allow for consideration of individual characteristics, even though those caught by the rule are likely to display a wide variety of the capabilities relevant to employment. It is an easy way of being selective that is based, in whole or in part, on stereotypical assumptions about the performance of older workers. In the result, it denies individuals equal opportunity to realize the economic benefits, dignity and self-satisfaction that come from being part of the work force.

Indeed, the federal government has already had legal advice saying, "compulsory-retirement provisions are vulnerable with the advent of section 15."

In late 1986 an Ontario Supreme Court judge (aged seventy) ruled that although mandatory retirement at sixty-five is discriminatory, it is nonetheless reasonable. However, it seems likely those against mandatory retirement will win the debate with the force of the Charter of Rights and Freedoms on their side. However, in terms of demographic trends, the debate seems more of an academic exercise. The economic realities of an aging population may make an extended working life a necessity rather than a right.

The main demographic trends are: (1) the aging of the "baby boom" generation; (2) increasing life expectancies; and (3) the declining birth rate. These demographic trends point to an increasing "dependency ratio." This means a greater proportion of the workforce would have to be supported by a shrinking working population. Currently there are six working-age Canadians (aged twenty to sixty-four) for each Canadian over age sixty-five; however in fifty years there will probably be only three working-age Canadians for each retired person — if sixty-five is maintained as the mandatory-retirement age.

For the immediate future, the trend to early retirement will undoubtedly continue because of economic realities. However, the aging population has implications for long-range human resource planning by employers. They must be prepared to tailor new and more flexible personnel policies and employee benefits to suit the needs of older workers.

In order to provide maximum benefits to organizations and to workers, employers should already be considering ways to deal with an aging workforce, such as:

- expansion of part-time or part-year employment;
- increased retraining for older workers;
- encouragement of lateral and downward moves;
- phased-in retirement programs;
- redesign of jobs;
- allowing employees to continue to accrue pension credits after age sixty-five;
- increased job-sharing.

11

What if I Don't Make it to Retirement?

If I can't take it with me when I go, I just ain't gonna go.

Eartha Kitt

NOW LET'S STEP BACK A LITTLE and consider some other issues. Most employers who provide pension plans for their employees also provide a whole range of other employee benefits:

- life insurance;
- health insurance;
- dental insurance;
- short- and long-term disability insurance;
- travel accident insurance.

Normally these programs complement the benefits provided by the federal and provincial governments. As well, the employer usually has certain objectives in mind:

- cost constraints;
- the need to make benefit plans cost-effective and tax-effective;
- the need for programs that are competitive with those offered by other companies in the same industry;
- flexibility in the plans;
- a requirement that employees make some contribution to help pay for the benefits; and
- the provision of a certain level of protection to the employees.

96

Death Benefits

Now, suppose you are an employer. You provide a pension plan to which employees do not contribute. You want to provide a death benefit for employees who might die while working for you. The big question is, how much of a death benefit do you want to provide? Equally important is the decision about how to provide the benefit — through the pension plan, the group life-insurance plan, or a combination of the two.

Here are some of the points for you to consider:

1. If you provide a group life-insurance benefit, the premium you pay for any coverage over $25,000 is a taxable benefit to your employees (i.e., it is added to their taxable incomes).
2. If you provide the benefit under the pension plan, the contribution is not a taxable benefit, but the ultimate benefit is taxable.
3. Revenue Canada imposes a limit on the maximum death benefit that can be provided under a pension plan.
4. If the death benefit is provided under the pension plan, it will be subject to the conditions imposed by the provincial pension authorities. In particular, this will affect your contributions as the employer.

Mainly because of this last issue, many employers with non-contributory pension plans provide no death benefit under the pension plan. Instead they provide the complete death benefit under group life insurance. Some employees believe, however, that if they have belonged to a pension plan for a number of years it owes them something, that if they die their beneficiaries should get a benefit from the plan.

The provincial pension authorities sympathize with both these positions. Most of the new legislation requires that a pension plan have a death benefit. If an employee dies, and he or she was vested in the plan, then the beneficiary is entitled to a benefit from the plan. In essence it is as if the employee had just left the employer to go to another job! The actuary will figure out how much the employee would have received as a pension if he or she had retired on the day he or she died. The value of that pension will be translated into a lump sum and paid to the beneficiary. Once again, remember that this legislation only became effective on January 1, 1987. It does not apply to any benefits earned before that date.

Under certain circumstances, both the Ontario and the federal governments are prepared to allow the death benefit to be reduced by any amount payable under a group insurance program. In this way the employer may be exempted from having to duplicate the death benefit.

The problem with providing the death benefit under the pension plan is that it runs contrary to the typical needs of an employee. Logic says that an individual who dies at age thirty and leaves a spouse with young children needs more life insurance protection than an individual who dies at age fifty when the children have probably grown up. The pension plan death benefit works the other way around. The thirty-year-old might have been in the plan for only four or five years. The value of the benefit would be very small because the employee is thirty-five or thirty-six years away from retirement. The fifty-year-old might have been in the plan for twenty-five years. Because the fifty-year-old is closer to retirement, the value of his or her death benefit could be as much as ten times larger than the thirty-year-old's.

It seems unlikely that pension plans will continue to be the major providers of pre-retirement death benefits. However, most employers will be required to include some death benefits under their pension plans.

The beneficiaries of employees who die while members of pension plans to which they had to contribute will always receive a refund of the employee contributions made, payable with interest.

Disability Benefits

Sometimes an employee who belongs to the pension plan becomes too ill or seriously injured to continue working. Many employers provide a continuing income to such employees (usually something less than full pay). The pension plan will usually also have a provision covering disabled employees. There are two standard approaches. Suppose your employer has a long-term disability (LTD) plan. If you become disabled, this plan will normally provide benefits to age sixty-five. The amount will be based on your earnings at the date you became disabled (typically between 50 percent and 70 percent). What happens when you turn sixty-five? Your pension payments will probably begin.

But if you were disabled at forty-five you can see some problems. If you are treated as if you left the company with a vested pension, the benefits you receive at age sixty-five will be based on service to age forty-five and your earnings at that time. Your pension could be very small. For this reason, many plans provide a credit for periods of disability. They count periods of disability as regular service for pension purposes; in other words, the pension you received at sixty-five would be based on all the years of service you would have had if you had been a healthy active employee until normal retirement age.

Inflation can also be a major concern for disabled employees. But few pension plans have dealt with the issue. Imagine that there are some years of high inflation between the time you become disabled and the time you turn sixty-five. Even though you are receiving credit for all those years of disability, ultimately your pension may still be very small because your pension will be based on your salary level when you became disabled. Normally in the case in which you were disabled at forty-five your salary would not increase and your final average salary for computing your pension would be very small.

Although Revenue Canada allows plans to increase the earnings base for disabled employees, this practice is still not widely followed. The provinces are silent on the subject. The best advice we can give you is this: if you do become disabled, be sure to remind your employer or your union that you still exist and that you have needs, too.

Obviously, employees who do not have LTD benefits are in a worse position. They still need an income, and the pension plan is the obvious source. For an employee aged fifty-five or more this is not a great problem. He or she can retire early and in many cases the plan will reduce or waive the reduction factors that would normally be applied. However, for a younger employee, the benefit probably will not be adequate.

The issue of providing a reasonable lifetime income to an individual who is totally and permanently disabled at a young age has not yet been addressed adequately by the private sector. But it may be unreasonable to expect an employer to take on such a huge financial obligation for an employee who may have been with the company only for a short period before becoming disabled.

12

How Will My Pension Be Paid?

*Buy an annuity cheap, and make your life
interesting to yourself and everyone else that
watches the speculation.*

Charles Dickens

REMEMBER HARRY'S FATHER? He had worked for the same company all his life. He retired in 1985 at the age of sixty-five with a pension of $30,000 a year payable for his life. After eight months he died and his pension payments stopped. Harry and his friends were appalled that all Harry's father had received from the company pension plan was a total of $20,000 (eight payments of $2,500) despite all his years of service. And Harry's mother was left high and dry. The employer explained that what had happened was a direct result of the pension option Harry's father had chosen. Harry's father could have lived to one hundred and received a total of more than $1 million in pension payments. Harry, however, was not impressed.

To understand what happened we must take a closer look at how annuities work. Harry's father had chosen a "life" annuity. He was entitled to an annuity payable for his life. It is really quite simple: each month that he was alive after he retired he received a pension payment. As soon as he died the payments stopped. Under current conditions a typical male who receives payments from an annuity at sixty-five is expected to live for about sixteen more years. A female at age sixty-five is expected to live for about twenty years.

Naturally there is a risk that an employee will not live as long as expected and could die very soon after retirement. For this reason, many pension plans pay annuities with a five-, ten-, or fifteen-year guarantee.

Let's look at the five-year guarantee. If the employee dies within the first five years after retirement, then the pension payments will be guaranteed to continue for the balance of the five-year period. If Harry's father had chosen the five-year guarantee his pension payments would have continued to Harry's mother or she could have received a lump sum representing the value of the outstanding payments. If Harry's father's pension had been guaranteed for ten years his wife would have continued to receive pension payments for nine years and four months after his death.

The five-year guarantee is the most common form of annuity under a contributory pension plan. The historical justification for this is the actuarial "rule of thumb" that the first five years of pension payments are financed by the employee's own contributions. After five years, the pension is financed by employer money.

A more sophisticated extension of this principle is the annuity that guarantees a refund of the employee's contributions. Suppose Harry's father had contributed $40,000 to the pension plan over his working lifetime. He died after receiving only $20,000, and so the guaranteed refund annuity would have paid $20,000 in this case. This type of annuity at least protects the employee's money.

The final type of annuity we will look at is called a "joint-and-last-survivor annuity." In its simplest form a 100 percent joint-and-last-survivor annuity provides for benefits to continue to the employee's spouse if the spouse outlives the employee. If Harry's father had been receiving a 100 percent joint-and-last-survivor pension, his wife would have continued to receive a pension of $30,000 per year for as long as she lived.

Sometimes under joint-and-last-survivor annuities the percentage continuing to the survivor is less than 100 percent of the initial pension. This scheme is based on the logic that one person should be able to live on less income than two. The most common formulae are 50 percent, 60 percent, 66⅔ percent, and 75 percent.

One last complication: the pension can be reduced on either

the death of the employee or the death of the spouse, or only on the death of the employee. Here are some examples based on a monthly pension of $100, and a 50 percent joint-and-last-survivor annuity.

1. Pension reducing on either death:
   a) The employee dies first. A pension of $50 a month continues to the spouse.
   b) The spouse dies first. A pension of $50 a month continues to the employee.

2. Pension reducing on employee's death:
   a) The employee dies first. A pension of $50 a month continues to the spouse.
   b) The spouse dies first. The pension of $100 a month continues to the employee.

The pension reducing on the employee's death is more common than a pension reducing on the first death. The traditional view was that the pension belonged to a male employee and that he was sharing it with his wife.

How does all this work when you retire? Can you choose whatever type of annuity you want and get the same amount of monthly pension? The answer is no. Why? Because different types of annuities are worth different amounts. From what we have said so far in this chapter, you may have figured out that an annuity payable for your life only is the cheapest option you can have. A 100 percent joint-and-last-survivor annuity guaranteed for fifteen years is the most expensive option.

At this point our friendly neighbourhood actuaries get involved again. They can assign values to all these different annuity forms, provided they know your age and the age of your spouse.

Suppose you are retiring from a defined-benefit pension plan. The plan will define the "normal form" of pension which is payable. Let's suppose that the normal form is a five-year guarantee and life after that.

Before you retire, the pension-plan administrator should provide you with a list of the pension options available to you. The option you select will be critical. Weigh all of the options carefully and discuss them with your spouse — unless you want your spouse to end up like Harry's mother.

Your pension options might look something like this:

Options	Amount of Monthly Pension
Your life only	$105
Normal form: five-year guarantee	100
Ten-year guarantee	95
50% joint-and-last-survivor, reducing on your death	90
100% joint-and-last-survivor	85

The options will have been calculated so that each is of equal value. Now, you have to decide which option is best for you or for you and your spouse.

If your spouse has his or her own pension income and will be quite comfortably off if you die, then the life-only option probably makes the most sense. If you are in poor health and have no insurance, then the 100 percent joint-and-last-survivor will be a better choice. Don't fall into the trap that Harry's father fell into. He selected the option that would pay him the largest pension without any thought for what his spouse would do if he died before she did.

A large number of elderly widows are in the same situation as Harry's mother, with no private pension income. As a result, one of the major issues in pension reform was the type of annuity that should be paid from a private pension plan. There appears to be almost unanimous agreement that the standard form of pension should be joint-and-last-survivor. This provides automatic protection for spouses, unless they sign a waiver indicating that they are aware of their entitlements but are prepared to accept another form of pension. There are still variations among the provinces regarding the percentage of pension that should be continued and the type of joint-and-last-survivor pension. The most common version is 60 percent continuation, reducing on the first death.

To protect the plan against possible charges of discrimination against single employees, it is still possible for a pension plan to keep the normal form as five-year guarantee and life thereafter. Married employees would then be required to take a reduced pension with a joint-and-last-survivor option.

Money-Purchase Plans

As usual, under money-purchase plans, the situation is much simpler. At retirement, employees have a lump sum available to buy a pension. Subject to the rules of the pension plan, they can buy any type of annuity that meets legislative requirements. The main rule to satisfy is that the benefit must be payable in the form of a life annuity. You cannot buy an annuity that pays a pension for ten years and then stops automatically. To avoid abuse, the maximum guarantee period is fifteen years.

Money-purchase plans, and even defined-benefit plans, produce one major problem in this area, the whole issue of "unisex mortality." This issue is discussed in detail in Chapter 13.

Early Retirement

Many of the options described in this section are available to employees who retire before or after normal-retirement age. For employees who retire early, there is another interesting option.

Remember we described the bridging benefit available under some plans? This compensated employees who retired early and were not yet eligible to receive Canada/Quebec Pension Plan or Old Age Security benefits. In other cases, employees can retire early and no bridging benefit is payable. In this situation the employee may be eligible for a level-pension option. the diagram on the next page shows how it works.

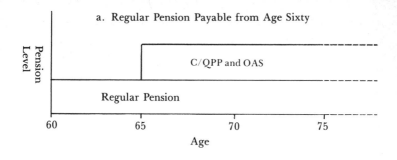

a. Regular Pension Payable from Age Sixty

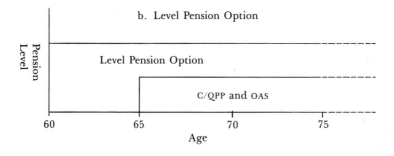

b. Level Pension Option

The level-pension option is calculated as a pension of equal value to the regular pension which literally "wraps around" the anticipated government pension to provide a level total pension. In practice the effect will not be quite as neat as the diagram suggests. In future, now that both the C/QPP will pay benefits from age sixty, it is likely that this option will lose popularity.

Commutation

Commutation is another of the pension buzz-words. What it really means is taking a cash lump sum instead of a pension. In Canada, tax legislation only permits commutation under specific situations. Either the individual is so sick that his or her life expectancy is dramatically reduced and there is no real chance of collecting sufficent benefits through a life annuity, or the amount of the pension is so small that it is not worth paying as a monthly income.

13

What if I'm a Woman?

Why can't a woman be more like a man?
Alan Jay Lerner

IN DISCUSSING THE PROBLEMS OF PRIVATE PENSION PLANS, we have referred to a number of issues as women's issues. These issues have had more of an impact on women than on men because, traditionally, more men than women were members of pension plans. The issues can be split into four categories.

1. *Death benefits.* This is the amount of benefit that continues to be paid to the spouse when the employee dies, either before or after retirement.

2. *Discrimination.* This issue concerns the possibility that individuals with similar positions at the same company could end up with significantly different pensions because one is male and the other female.

3. *Family law issues.* There is concern that a spouse could lose benefits because of the definition of "spouse" used in the pension plan or because the marriage ends.

4. *Maternity leave.* This issue concerns whether service in the plan should be credited during maternity leave.

Let's look at each of these issues more closely.

Death Benefits

As we saw in Chapter 11, most provinces have taken steps to improve the level of death benefits paid under private pension plans. If an employee dies before retiring, the pension plan will pay the spouse a benefit equal in value to the pension that the member had earned. If the employee dies after retirement, the spouse will receive a pension equal to 60 percent of the amount being paid to the member, unless the spouse deliberately waives this right. These rules are a major improvement over the "bad old days" when an employee about to retire could choose the form of pension which paid the highest amount possible, without any thought for his or her spouse.

Discrimination

There are several ways in which a pension plan could discriminate against women. A plan could provide different eligibility rules for men and women. Historically many plans admitted men earlier than women, based on the logic that men were in the plan for life whereas women worked only until they were ready to start a family.

A pension plan might provide different normal-retirement ages for men and women. In Britain it is still common for women to retire at age sixty and men at age sixty-five. The logic behind such a custom is highly suspect. After all, we know that, on average, women outlive men.

Thanks to human rights legislation, such examples of discrimination are now rare. But there are two areas in which discrimination by sex still exists.

Many women are still paid less than men for doing substantially the same work. In any pension plan in which benefits are based on earnings this will obviously result in a lower benefit being paid to women. The solution to this problem should come from "pay equity" legislation.

The other area involves mortality. It is well known that women live longer than men. On average a woman retiring at age sixty-five will outlive a man retiring at the same age by about four years.

This distinction has been reflected in the annuity rates offered by insurance companies. As a result men can be paid a better monthly income than women because of their shorter life expectancy. Therefore, if a man and a woman both have identical working careers, belong to a money-purchase plan, and retire at the same age, on the same date, they will receive different pensions. This seems to be patently unfair. But what is the alternative?

If we want to provide equal pensions to men and women, women will have to pay more into the pension plan. That doesn't seem fair either.

The simplistic answer is for insurance companies to change their current practice. If all insurance companies charged annuity rates based on the combined mortality of males and females, the problem would be solved. However, without legislation, insurance companies won't act. No insurer would take the first step since that step would cost the insurer more.

This issue may take years to resolve. One side argues that the greater longevity of women is a statistical fact that should be reflected in the rates charged. The other side argues that society could be subdivided many ways: by race, by colour, by smoker/non-smoker, by sex. Some subdivisions are socially acceptable, others are not. Discrimination by sex is not.

The question of the amount of pension to be paid from a money-purchase pension plan is the most important issue in this debate. However, there are other minor issues that affect defined-benefit plans. The actuarial factors used to calculate the value of different payment options at retirement should all, in theory, reflect the different mortality of males and females. In practice, it is far easier for an employer to use factors that do not vary by sex in these circumstances.

Family Law

Let's look at Jack and Andrea, who have been married for many years. During their marriage, Jack was working for a company that provided a pension plan. Andrea worked at home, raised the children, and had no taxable income. Just before Jack's retirement the couple were divorced. Andrea will receive no pension in retirement apart from the basic Old Age Security and the Guaranteed Income Supplement, if she is eligible. Jack will receive the full amount of his pension. Is this fair?

It is because of situations like this that the concept of credit-splitting was developed. The concept is simple: the husband and wife as a unit make contributions to their family. Although one receives a taxable income and the other does not, their real contributions to the marriage are equal. Any assets they accumulate are shared assets, including pension benefits. All of this sounds logical until we ask the question "How do you split pension credits?"

The most straightforward approach to this problem is to wait until the payments are actually made to the employee, and then to divert a portion to the ex-spouse. An interesting situation arises if the ex-spouse dies before the first payment is due. Should the payments be part of the spouse's estate or would the whole pension revert to the employee?

A second approach is to calculate the present value of the pension at the date of separation. Both spouses would be entitled to half the value. But who would decide the actual pension that each would receive?

These issues were brought sharply into focus by the new Family Law Act in Ontario which was implemented on March 1, 1986. The topic is too complicated for detailed discussion here, but the major point is, pensions do form a part of the family assets to be divided on divorce. Be sure to ask your lawyer about pension assets if you are in the process of getting a separation or divorce.

Maternity Leave

One of the aims of women's groups is to have maternity leave treated as a paid leave of absence. If this happens, it would be natural to receive credit under the pension plan for that period.

Since maternity leave is normally taken without pay, there are a variety of ways of dealing with the pension plan. If the pension plan is non-contributory, many plans credit the period of maternity leave. If the plan is contributory, normally the pension benefits are only credited if employees make up their missed contributions when they return to the job.

To summarize, many of the issues which make pensions appear unfair to women are byproducts of a general system in society which is unfair, rather than deliberate features of plan design. Change will come as society recognizes the equality of men and women. However, it will not come overnight.

14

What About Inflation?

Inflation: when the buck doesn't stop anywhere.

Orben's Current Comedy

INFLATION PROTECTION IS THE SINGLE MOST EXPENSIVE and most contentious issue in pension reform. We have left the discussion until late in the book because you need a good knowledge of pensions to understand what is involved.

Inflation has a number of effects on pension plans. It is such a serious concern because many pension plans were designed in an era when inflation was not such an important issue. Earlier we saw the effect inflation has on the value of a pension if you leave your job before retirement and you are vested. Pensions earned for fairly long periods of employment can become almost worthless by the time an employee is ready to retire. We have also seen that inflation severely reduces the effectiveness of flat-benefit and career-average pension plans and frequent updates are needed to maintain purchasing power.

Only final-/best-average pension plans, which base the total pension on earnings close to retirement, provide any guaranteed protection for the employee. Even in these plans, a long averaging period can greatly reduce the value of the pension. Consider Sharon, whose earnings over the last ten years of her employment are shown on the next page.

Age	Earnings
55	$30,000
56	33,000
57	36,000
58	39,000
59	42,000
60	45,000
61	48,000
62	51,000
63	54,000
64	57,000

Sharon's average earnings over the last ten years would be $43,500. Seventy percent of her final-average earnings would be $30,450, only about half of her final earnings.

Money-purchase plans provide protection against inflation if the rate of return the assets earned is greater than the inflation rate from year to year. However, as we noted before, in this situation the employee bears all of the risk.

Although inflation has an impact on how much pension an employee will receive, it has a much bigger impact once the employee retires. The debate on this issue has been especially heated because some pensions are already fully indexed. Both the Canada/Quebec Pension Plan and the Old Age Security pensions increase in line with the Consumer Price Index. The federal public-service pension plan also provides indexed pensions.

The private sector argues that it is unreasonable to expect employers to sign a "blank cheque" for retired employees. Unlike the public sector, there is no guarantee that a private company will remain in business and a private company does not have the assured financial base of taxation to cover operating expenses. At the same time, if pension plans do nothing to increase the pensions of past employees then they will make a profit from these individuals. Why? Because, frequently, when inflation rates are high, rates of return are also high and the pension-plan assets grow in value with no corresponding increase in the liabilities.

Suppose under a pension plan the actuary has assumed the future investment-return rate as 7 percent a year. The liability for employees who have retired and are receiving pensions is $10 million. If the rate of return in a particular year is 17 percent, then the plan has made a profit of 10 percent of $10 million, or $1 million. Who gets the $1 million? This is referred to as excess interest. There are at least three possibilities:

1. The company could increase the pensions of all the retired employees by 10 percent.
2. The company could increase benefits for current employees.
3. The company could keep the $1 million in the plan so that in some later year it would not have to make its usual contribution.

If you were the employer, what would you do? Option 3 saves you money, option 2 benefits your existing employees, option 1 fulfils a nebulous moral responsibility to retired employees. During the recent years of high inflation many employers used a compromise. They made ad hoc increases to pensions for retired employees and used the rest of the profit from their investments for other purposes.

In response to public pressure, in the early 1980s a specific formula was proposed to ensure that a large percentage of this "excess interest" would be used to increase pensions. The government supported this approach. For them it was an attractive compromise between the practices in the private and public sectors.

The private-sector response to excess interest was generally negative. Although a number of organizations had been using a modified excess-interest formula for years, most rejected the concept. They had several arguments against it:

- Governments should not introduce such legislation retroactively by applying the excess-interest formula to benefits already earned. The logic here was that, if the employer had known that benefits were going to be indexed, he would have cut back the level of benefits.
- It is not right to apply one formula to all pension plans because they each earn very different rates of return. This argument was strengthened by the fact that the formula pro-

posed could not be matched with certainty by any pension plan.

- If retired employees get increases in the good years, they should also get decreases in the bad years.

By late 1983 it was no great surprise to find that the concept of excess interest had been dropped from pension-reform proposals. In its place was a simpler proposal to increase pensions that were being paid, after the date of the new legislation, by 60 percent of the Consumer Price Index annually. This indexing was to be tied to the "ability to pay" by limiting the annual pension increase in line with two new indices, one based on anticipated investment return, the other based on average wages.

The 1984 federal budget supported the notion of indexing in line with 60 percent of increases in the Consumer Price Index. While these proposals had evoked great passion from employers in the mid-1970s, by 1984, there was a general consensus that something had to be done about inflation protection for Canada's pensioners.

Since 1984 inflation rates have fallen dramatically and the cost of living is no longer the political issue it was. However, the issue of indexing pensions in payment has not died. In March 1989, the Ontario government released proposals for the mandatory inflation protection of pension benefits. By this writing, an election had intervened and no legislation had been forthcoming. It seems likely that, in the not too distant future, some form of inflation protection will be mandated in Ontario. Once that happens, we predict other provinces will follow. In the meantime, a number of labour contracts have been negotiated with inflation protection in the pension plans. It clearly will continue to be an issue and it will continue to be central in the debate over refunds of surplus.

Rates of Return

An issue of concern for many employees lies in the rate of return credited to their contributions. In the early days of pension plans, many plans were funded through a group annuity which only credited a nominal rate of interest, such as 2.5 percent or 3 percent, to employee contributions. In the 1980s, some plans continued to pay such low rates, even in years of very high inflation. Some employers just hadn't got around to changing the rate. However, many employers justified the low rate they were paying. Their logic was that, in a defined-benefit pension plan, the benefit paid at retirement is not influenced by the amount of interest credited to employee contributions. The main loser is the employee who leaves a pension plan before he or she is vested, not a high priority in the historical scheme of things.

In this new era of pensions with shorter vesting periods, increased portability, and improved standards of disclosure, this question has gained a higher profile. Many employees equate the rate credited to their contributions with the rate of return actually earned by the fund. Others have compared the position under their pension plan with the rates of return they could earn in their own Registered Retirement Savings Plan, guaranteed investment certificates, or Canada Savings Bonds. They have concluded, often incorrectly, that it is not worth belonging to a pension plan.

After pension reform most provinces have introduced provisions which require plans to base the rate of interest on either the actual earnings of the fund assets or an economic indicator. The most common indicator used is the average of the five year personal fixed term chartered bank deposit rate (CANSIM series B14045) over a reasonably current period. This rate has the advantage of always being positive, whereas the fund rate can clearly be negative in some years.

15

Who Looks After the Assets?

There is never an instant's truce between virtue and vice. Goodness is the only investment that never fails.

Henry David Thoreau

IN CHAPTER 6, WE DESCRIBED THE PRE-FUNDING of pension benefits. It is one of the essential features of a private pension plan in Canada. Public plans like the Old Age Security program can rely on the future inflow of tax dollars to pay the promised benefits. Unless the taxpayers rebel, we will all receive our Old Age Security. There are no such guarantees in the private sector.

Suppose you are a member of a pension plan that has no pre-funding. Every year the employer makes a contribution that is just enough to meet the pension payments for that year and the administrative expenses. Many things could go wrong. The company could go bankrupt. Who would pay the outstanding pensions? The number of retired employees could increase compared with the number of active employees. Could the employer afford to keep paying pensions out of the current operating budget?

It is clear that, in order to make private plans a workable proposition, the employer must have a device which allows him to smooth costs over time and to anticipate future significant events that could affect the cost of the plan. This device involves setting up a pension fund to be used at a future date to pay the pensions. The process has been compared to running a bath with the plug out. It is possible to adjust the taps so that the amount of water slowly increases, slowly decreases, or stays constant. The water in the bath-tub is equivalent to the assets in the pension fund.

The main issue is how to invest the pension assets of a typical pension fund. We will try to keep the discussion as simple as possible, so you don't have to be an investment expert.

There are various classes of assets in which a pension fund can invest:

- common stocks;
- bonds;
- mortgages;
- short-term investments;
- real estate.

Each of these classes of investments has different characteristics. Common stocks historically have given the highest rates of return over long periods of time. However, the value of any particular common stock can vary significantly from day to day. This is called "volatility." Short-term investments have the least volatility. Non-chequing savings accounts are a good example. The rates of interest don't vary widely but this class of investment has historically given the lowest long-term rates of return.

Remember Chapter 6, on funding, in which we looked at the example of Harry March saving for his trailer? He had twenty years to save for the trailer. One issue we did not discuss was the choice of investments he should make. What would you do if the choice was yours? Common stocks might look very attractive for the first few years, when you would want the maximum possible rate of return. Now, suppose you are one year away from buying the trailer. It would be pretty risky to invest your whole fund in common stocks. The bottom might drop out of the stock market just as you were about to buy the trailer. Perhaps you would decide to invest in a one-year guaranteed-investment certificate. You would know exactly how much you could expect to have at the end of the twenty years.

Who decides how the money in your pension plan will be invested? Usually it is the job of the pension fund or investment manager guided by and watched over by your employer. The fund manager selects a mix of investment classes suitable for your pension plan. The investment mix will depend on several factors, such as the type of plan, the average age of the members, the fund manager's view of the economy, the employer's attitude to risk, and the involvement of the employees. everyone involved in the decision-making process for a pension fund has what is known as a "fiduciary responsibility". This means that the financial well-being of the fund's assets must be one of the primary goals of the sponsor, the administrator, the trustee and custodian, the investment manager and any external agent working for the fund.

The second part of the investment manager's job is to pick the individual investments within each asset category. In this case, the investment manager is guided more by basic investment principles than by the characteristics of the particular plan.

What is the difference between investing a pension fund and investing a similar fund for an individual? There are three answers:

1. Normally there is a much longer time-frame in the investment of pension funds. A contribution may be made for an individual aged twenty, and that same individual may live and receive pension benefits to age eighty.

2. Pension funds are tax exempt. Investment decisions which might make sense for a fund that is taxed could be quite meaningless for a pension fund. For example, an individual might prefer an investment which gives him capital gains rather than one that gives him investment income. For a pension fund it is irrelevant since both are tax-free.

3. Pension funds are subject to provincial and federal rules. Because the pensions of individuals depend on the value of the pension investments, it is essential that the funds not be invested frivolously or used for some other purpose.

There are rules governing the quality of the investments and the proportion of each asset category which may be included in your pension fund. There are many allowable categories including common stocks, bonds, short-term investments, mortgages and real estate. Each province has specific regulations.

Historically one of the most contentious rules covered investment in foreign assets. Not more than 10 percent of a pension fund could be invested in non-Canadian investments. This was a source of great frustration to some investment managers who saw tremendous potential in the United States and elsewhere.

In the federal budget of 1985, Minister of Finance Michael Wilson proposed an attractive arrangement to help solve this problem. The government wanted to encourage investment in small and developing businesses. To do this they dangled a carrot. An extra $3 would be permitted to be invested in foreign investments for every $1 invested in Canadian small business.

Proposed Federal tax legislation increases the maximum foreign content on a graduated basis over the five years starting in 1990 by two percent increments annually to a new maximum of 20 percent by January 1, 1994.

All in all, pension plan investment is a complex business conducted by experts. Unfortunately, some are more expert than others!

Great pressure is placed on the investment manager when employees must contribute to the pension plan. Employees always compare the rate of return in the pension plan against the rate they could have obtained from their favourite RRSP. This can be an unfair comparison when we remember that pension managers have a long-term time horizon while most individuals have short-term investment objectives.

These days, most pension funds are invested in either segregated funds or pooled funds. A segregated fund is just what it sounds like. The assets of the plan are held separately and invested by the money manager. But suppose that your fund only contains $500,000? It would be difficult for a manager to invest this amount and buy the right selection of the different investment classes. For this reason, many managers establish pooled funds, pools of investments in different asset classes. For example, a pooled bond fund might contain a wide selection of different types of bonds — federal, provincial, corporate, and municipal — with varying periods to maturity. Any particular pension fund can then buy units of the various pooled funds offered by the money manager.

In defined-contribution (money-purchase) plans, the investment decisions are often left to you as the plan member. You can choose between a variety of pooled funds and your choice can be changed at regular intervals.

Recent legislation in Ontario and Quebec has required plan sponsors to develop and document specific guidelines for investments and goals for performance which must be filed with the provincial authorities.

Besides the question of who invests the funds, there are two additional questions. Who holds the assets which are invested? Who is responsible for making sure the assets are used properly? Now we have to look at the roles of the custodian and the trustee.

The role of the custodian is quite simple. Some institution has to be responsible for holding the actual assets. This can be a bank, an insurance company, or a trust company.

The role of trustee must be provided by a trust company or "a group of individuals at least three of whom reside in Canada and one of whom must be independent to the extent that he is neither a significant shareholder, partner, proprietor nor an employee of a participating employer." (In other words someone without any axe to grind!) Alternatively the pension plan may be funded through an insurance contract. Whoever provides the service, the key point is that some organization or group of people is responsible for making sure that the assets of the pension fund are invested in line with legislation and are used only for purposes covered in the pension plan document and the trust agreement/insurance contract.

16

What Is Integration?

*Work is doing what you now enjoy for the sake
of a future which you clearly see and desire.
Drudgery is doing under strain what you don't
now enjoy and for no end that you can now
appreciate.*

Richard C. Cabot

SUPPOSE WE LIVED IN ANOTHER WORLD, one in which there were
no government pension programs of any kind. What effect would
this have on private pensions?

For a start, it would have a major impact on your attitude. If
you reached retirement with no pension arranged, there would be
no money for you to live on. What effect would this have? It would
likely lead to a continuation of the extended family. Certainly it
would lead to a greater demand for employer pension plans.

Imagine that you were a member of such a plan. You are
required to contribute 5 percent of your annual pay to the plan
and at retirement you will receive a pension of 2 percent of your
final-average pay per year of plan membership.

Push your imagination a little farther. Suppose that the government now introduces a national pension program under which
you and your employer both contribute 2 percent of pay. The benefit at retirement is equal to 1 percent of final-average pay per
year of service. What would this do to your private pension plan?
There are three possibilities:

1. You might not want to contribute 7 percent of your annual pay to two pension plans.

2. Your employer might not be able to bear the financial responsibility for a 2 percent contribution to the government plan and the cost of the private plan.

3. A benefit of 3 percent of final-average pay per year of membership (1 percent from the government plan and 2 percent from the private plan) might result in a very large pension. An individual retiring with thirty-five years of membership would receive a pension equal to 105 percent of his final-average pay. He or she would be better off retired than working!

There is a solution to these three issues. It is called "integration." First, your employer might reduce your contribution to his plan by the 2 percent of annual pay you will contribute to the government plan. Second, your employer might reduce your pension from the plan by the 1 percent of final-average pay per year of membership you will receive from the government plan. The overall effect of the introduction of the government plan is then zero. Your contributions and benefits are unchanged in total. But they are now split between two plans.

What relevance does this have to you as a Canadian? A great deal if you had been a member of a private pension plan on January 1, 1966. That's the date the Canada/Quebec Pension Plan was introduced. All employers with pension plans had to face the three situations described above. The solutions they found led to much of the complexity of modern private pension plans.

Some employers decided not to make changes to their plans. Maybe their plans were non-contributory and the benefits were quite modest. They may have felt that the Canada/Quebec Pension Plan would complement their plan and would, in total, provide a reasonable benefit. These plans are said to be "stacked," because the benefits they provide are stacked on top of the benefits from government plans. Flat-dollar pension programs are good examples of stacked plans.

Direct-Offset Integration

Other employers used "direct offset" integration. This sounds very complicated, but is, in fact, the method used in our example. The employee's contribution and the plan benefits are reduced by the contribution requirement and benefits payable under the Canada/Quebec Pension Plan.

For contributions this is fairly straightforward. If the original employee contribution was 5 percent of pay then the integrated contribution would be 5 percent of pay less the employee contribution to the Canada/Quebec Pension Plan. Now, however, this is complicated by the decision to increase the required contributions to the C/QPP from the 1986 level of 3.6 percent (1.8 percent from both the employer and the employee) to its ultimate level of 7.6 percent (3.8 percent from both the employer and the employee). If you are a member of an integrated contributory pension plan then your contribution to that plan will decrease as your contributions to the C/QPP increase. If your contribution formula changed in 1987 this may be the reason. Your employer switched to a new approach in order to avoid a reduction in your contributions.

Direct-offset integration of your pension benefits involves a number of interesting questions. For example, is it fair to offset the whole C/QPP pension from an individual who is retiring with only short service in the pension plan? No, it is not. Suppose you retired from a 2 percent final-average pension plan in 1990 with ten years of credited service and a final-average salary of $30,000. Your pension would be $6,000 per year (2 percent × 10 × $30,000) which is $500 a month. The maximum C/QPP pension payable in 1990 was $577.08 per month. Complete integration would wipe out your whole pension. Because of this obvious unfairness most plans spread the offset over the employee's working lifetime. The new rules will not allow your employer to reduce the pension you have earned for one year of service by more than one-thirty-fifth of the C/QPP pension. In the above example, the maximum offset would be $577.08 × 10 years ÷ 35 or $164.88. The integrated pension from your employer would then be $335.12 per month ($500.00 less $164.88).

Is it fair to offset the full C/QPP benefit from an employee retiring with a low rate of pay? Again, the answer is no. Suppose you retired from a 2 percent final-average pension plan in 1990 with thirty-five years of credited service and a final-average salary of $15,000. Your pension would be $10,500 per year (2 percent × 35 × $15,000) which is $875 a month. If we applied the maximum offset of $577.08 then this pension would be reduced to $297.92 per month. To avoid this type of unfairness most employers base the offset on a realistic estimate of the C/QPP pension that the employee will receive. In this case the estimate would be $3,750 per year (25 percent of $15,000 or $312.50 per month. The integrated pension from your employer would be $562.50 per month ($875.00 less $312.50).

Is it fair to increase the offset for retired employees each year in line with changes in the C/QPP benefit? As you know, C/QPP pensions are increased each year in line with changes in the Consumer Price Index. If your private pension benefit was not indexed and the offset kept increasing you would finally end up with only the C/QPP and no private pension benefits. Provincial rules forbid this type of adjustment.

Is it fair to include the Old Age Security pension in the calculation of the offset? Consider the basic logic of integration. It is to provide a combined pension from the two government plans and from a private plan that satisfies certain objectives. So we might say, "Sure, add in OAS. It's payable to everyone." But if we remember that the OAS is funded through tax revenues and is not paid for directly by either the employer or the employees we might say, "How dare they reduce my pension just because the government pays me my Old Age Security?" The latter view has won out, at least in Ontario, where no private plan can reduce benefits earned after January 1, 1987, by OAS benefits.

Finally, one last question. Is it right to offset the whole C/QPP pension from a non-contributory pension plan? If we take the view that the C/QPP is funded, half by your contributions and half by your employer's then we might argue that a non-contributory pension plan has no business offsetting the half of the C/QPP that you are paying for. If you go back to the overall philosophy, that the two plans have to work together to provide you with a reasonable pension, then it can be justified. The jury is still out on this one.

Step-Rate Integration

An alternative approach to integration is called the "step-rate approach." This approach recognizes the significance of earnings above the Year's Maximum Pensionable Earnings (YMPE) compared to earnings below the YMPE used to calculate contributions and benefits under the C/QPP. An example of a step-rate contribution formula might be 2.5 percent of pay up to the YMPE and 5 percent of pay above the YMPE. This approach overcomes a problem mentioned earlier. As the C/QPP contribution rate rises slowly to 7.6 percent of pay, the employee's required rate of contribution to a private plan does not alter if the plan uses a step-rate formula.

The use of the step-rate approach also simplifies benefit integration. In a career-average pension plan with required employee contributions of 2.5 percent of pay up to the YMPE and 5 percent above, a typical benefit per year of service would be 40 percent of contributions or 1 percent of pay up to the YMPE and 2 percent above. Notice that this approach simply sidesteps all the previous questions. It is fair for short-service employees. For lower-paid employees it provides a total benefit based on the lower rate of accrual. Because there is no explicit offset, it avoids many of the emotional issues that arise with direct offsets.

This chapter has concentrated upon defined-benefit pension plans because integration is not such a major issue for defined-contribution (money-purchase) plans. Although employee contributions can still be integrated using either a direct-offset or step-rate approach, the ultimate benefit cannot be integrated since there is no target benefit to aim for. The contributions just accumulate to whatever level the fund rates of return take them to.

Finally, we should remember that pension plans provide not only retirement benefits but also death and disability benefits. Historically the C/QPP death benefit was so small that it was not integrated with the private-plan death benefit. As these benefits become more significant because of changes in legislation we may well see some integration in this area.

The C/QPP disability benefits can be either stacked on or integrated with the private-plan benefits. However, as we discussed in Chapter 11, these disability benefits are most frequently provided through an insured long-term disability plan.

17

The Write Stuff

Wherefore are these things hid?
Shakespeare

OUR MAIN REASON FOR WRITING THIS BOOK was our concern that most employees do not understand their pension plans, despite the enormous sums of money that are contributed annually by employees and employers.

Why is this? Are pension plans really that complicated? Or is there some conspiracy afoot to confuse the general public?

In their purest form, pension plans are not really that difficult to understand. Consider the following plans:

1. Every year you contribute 5 percent of your pay into a pension fund. Your employer matches this contribution. When you leave the company for whatever reason, all the contributions made on your behalf plus interest will be used to buy you an annuity payable beginning at age sixty-five.

2. If you retire from the company with at least ten years of service you will receive a pension payable for life equal to 70 percent of your pay at your date of retirement.

Both of these plans are simple enough. By now you should recognize the first plan is a money-purchase plan with immediate vesting. The second plan is a defined-benefit, non-contributory, final-pay plan with no vesting, no disability, and no death benefits.

There are several reasons why pension plans are not always this simple. The employer may want to build in more flexibility and control costs. Legislation imposes minimum standards for death, disability, and termination. Employment standards require the removal of any discriminatory rules. Pension plans do not exist in a vacuum. They co-exist with government programs and individual arrangements.

The one issue that causes difficulties for many people is the problem of understanding an annuity. We have known employees who saw the amount of their annual pension and thought that that amount was all they would receive from the plan. They could not relate to the concept of this amount being paid year after year. Most of us are used to dealing with cash. Given the choice between an annuity and a cash option, most of us would choose the cash, even though the annuity may have a far greater value. This is the well-known phenomenon of a bird in the hand being worth two in the bush!

Would Canadians relate better to pension plans if they provided cash rather than an income? Probably yes.

Is There a Conspiracy To Confuse?

Most of us enjoy surrounding a topic that we understand with enough jargon to make it incomprehensible to other people. It gives us a feeling of power, perhaps, or of belonging. There is certainly an element of this in the world of pensions. Consultants and insurance companies who write employee handbooks frequently use some form of mock legalese and succeed in clouding the major issues.

There is no need for this. Certainly there are legal implications for pension handbooks. The material should not be so vague that it can be misinterpreted. However, handbooks do not have to be based on excerpts from the plan document. Their prime requirement is to communicate clearly the major features and benefits of the plan.

Employers are not always anxious to provide attractive, clear material for their employees for a number of reasons. Good communications material is more expensive than poor communications material. An outstanding communications program for voluntary programs could lead to a large increase in participation and this could cause a financial embarrassment to the employer. There is also a feeling among many employers that if employees know more than the bare minimum they will want an increasing voice in the operation of the plan. The company may feel that the design, funding, and investment of the pension plan are a corporate responsibility.

Despite these problems, more and more employers are making a real effort to explain pension programs to employees. If you are in a pension plan you will have received a summary of the plan either when you were hired or when you were eligible to join the plan. You have probably also received pension statements showing the benefits you can expect from the plan.

The impetus for this trend was provided by provincial legislation. After all, there is not much point making rules about pension entitlements, vesting, and funding if the employer can skirt the whole issue by not telling his employees about the pension plan.

The new rules cover three types of communication. First, the material describing the basic plan rules must be distributed at the time you are hired or at least thirty days before the date you are eligible to join the plan. You must also be informed if the plan is being changed in any way. And remember, it cannot be changed so as to take away any benefits you have already earned.

Second, additional material must be made available to you if you ask for it. This includes recent actuarial reports, investment reports, the actual text of the pension-plan document, and copies of recent correspondence between your employer and the government authorities. Most of this material is best read as a cure for insomnia. But it is certainly your right to ask for it.

Finally, regular statements must provide personal information to you. These statements will include your date of birth, date of hire, and date of joining the plan. Check them carefully. If they are wrong it could affect your eligibility for benefits or the actual amounts that you will receive. You will also be provided with information on the pension you have earned to date (normally called your "accrued pension"), the pension you can expect at retirement (normally called your "projected pension"), and the benefits you will receive if you quit, die, or become disabled. Later in this book we will show you how to use this information to do some planning for your retirement. The statements should be provided once a year to active members and also when you leave your employer for whatever reason.

One of the major problems in providing these statements is that of striking a balance between what is realistic and what is understandable. Suppose you are a thirty-year-old earning $30,000 a year, and that you are a member of a pension plan that provides a pension of 1 percent of your final-average pay at retirement (age sixty-five). If your salary increases at 5 percent per year, then your final-average pay will be approximately $143,000. If your salary increases at 10 percent per year, then your final-average pay will be approximately $633,000. The projected pensions would be $50,000 and $221,500 respectively. Do these numbers really mean anything? Probably not. They are unrealistic in today's environment. For this reason, employers have opted to base pension projections on current earnings. You would see a projected pension of $10,500 ($30,000 × 1 percent × 35). This approach also saves employers the problem of having to indicate to you what your future salary increases might be.

Another problem that must be faced is the preparation of statements for employees close to retirement. If your pension is based on your average earnings in the last five years of employment and you are now aged sixty-four, then it is dangerous to base your projected pension on your current earnings.

Look at this example:

Age	Pay
60	$30,000
61	33,000
62	36,000
63	39,000
64	42,000

In this case the final average salary is $36,000 per year. The salary at age sixty-four is $42,000. You would be very upset if the pension you actually received at retirement was less than the amount shown in your most recent pension statement.

Although the impetus for improved communications has come from the governments, many employers have also realized that, given the cost of pension plans, they should be providing more information to their employees and "selling the plan."

We have seen companies print their benefit statements in all kinds of intriguing formats to try to reach their employees. Statements disguised as soup cans, computer diskettes, and slide-rules are just examples of what can be done.

Companies are now expanding their horizons. Audio-visual presentations are becoming more common. Now companies are moving to computer technology to help them. If you can push a button at Disney World to see which restaurants serve Chinese food, you should be able to push a button at work to see the basic details of your pension plan. Computerized networks will allow you to obtain your own benefit statements when you want them, just as you can now walk into your bank and print out a statement of your chequing account.

Technology will also enhance pension-administration systems. Gone are the days when it took a month to have your benefit entitlement calculated. In your company this information may now be available instantly from your personnel department.

18

What if the Plan Terminates Before I Do?

> *But in this world nothing can be said to be*
> *certain, except death and taxes.*
>
> Benjamin Franklin

IF YOU ARE A MEMBER OF A PENSION PLAN, have you ever wondered what would happen if your employer decided to end the plan? Would you lose all of your pension? Or maybe only receive a small fraction of what you were entitled to? If you have read Chapter 6, on funding, you might wonder what there is to worry about. Surely, every year your employer and you contribute enough to pay for the benefits earned in that year. The plan should be fully funded at any time, meaning that the assets should cover the liabilities for pensions earned to date. How can there be a problem?

In actual fact, serious deficits can arise. There could be "adverse experience" under the plan. Things just may not work out the way the actuary expected. Maybe the rates of return were not as good as the actuary anticipated. Maybe salaries increased far more than was expected, creating larger liabilities. A large number of plan members may have taken advantage of favourable early-retirement provisions.

Consider a very simple case: a final-average pension plan in which assets are $10 million and liabilities are $10 million. The actuary has assumed a long-term rate of return of 6 percent per year and salary increases of 5 percent per year. If in a given year the rate of return is zero and salary increases are 15 percent, there will be an asset deficiency of $600,000 (the investment income we would have expected) and an excess liability of $1 million (because of the high salary increases). The funding will be in the hole to the tune of $1.6 million.

Then again, maybe the employer improves benefits. Suppose you are in a flat-dollar benefit plan where the benefit is $6 per month per year of service. Assets are $6 million and so are liabilities. Now suppose that, as a result of negotiations, the $6 benefit is increased to $10. Overnight the liability becomes $10 million while the assets remain at $6 million. There is a deficit of $4 million.

Another reason a deficit can arise is if contributions are not made. The first two types of deficiencies can affect any plan. Indeed, few plans have not had a deficiency at one time or another. However, some situations have arisen solely because the employer broke the rules that apply to pension plans. Suppose you are an employer with a contributory pension plan who is experiencing financial problems. It would be very tempting to stop making the required contributions to the pension plan. It might even be tempting to keep taking your employees' contributions but not to pay them into the pension fund. Who would notice?

Previously we mentioned that employers are required to file an annual information return with the province in which their pension plan is registered. Analysts for the province compare the contributions made to the plan against the contributions recommended in the most recent actuarial valuation. They would notice if the contributions were not being paid in. However, an unscrupulous employer could probably get away with this tactic for a couple of years before pressure was brought to bear.

What happens if a pension plan is in a deficit position and the plan is ended? Normally, annuities are bought for employees who are already retired or who are eligible to retire under the plan. Because annuity purchase rates are usually calculated on higher rates of interest than actuarial liabilities, even a plan which is apparently in deficit may have enough assets to buy immediate or deferred annuities for all members. If there are not enough assets, the younger members will have their benefits reduced.

Several years ago Ontario introduced a Pension Guarantee Fund to protect the benefits of employees whose pension plan might end.

The rationale for this fund was largely political. Employees (and that means voters!) were worried about the possibility of bankruptcy of even some major Canadian employers. The fund was established to put employees at ease.

The Ontario Pension Guarantee Fund charges employers a premium based on the unfunded liability under their pension plans. The logic is that if a plan has an unfunded liability it is less likely to be able to meet its obligations than a plan that has a surplus.

The fund does not cover plans that have been in existence for less than three years or amendments that have been in force for less than three years. It does, however, provide a measure of security to plan members. At the same time it does not provide an open invitation to employers to terminate underfunded plans. The Ontario Pension Benefits Act makes it quite clear that the payment of pensions upon plan termination remain the obligation of the employer, whether or not a payment under the fund is made.

None of these issues should ever arise with a defined-contribution plan. On plan termination every member is entitled to his or her contribution account.

The protection of employees has been strengthened, in most provinces, by requiring the actuary to produce a regular solvency valuation. This valuation shows what would happen if the plan were wound-up. If a deficit is disclosed then corrective action must be taken immediately.

19

Who Owns the Surplus Anyway?

Now is the winter of our discontent.

Shakespeare

ANOTHER OF THE HOT PENSION ISSUES of the 1980s was the question of refunds of surplus to employers who demonstrated that their pension plans had surpluses. Let's look at two extreme cases to see why this is such a controversial topic.

In case one, a company has a compulsory, contributory, career-average pension plan. Until 1986 it credited 3 percent interest on employee contributions. It never updated the past-service benefit entitlements, although inflation had considerably reduced their value. Not surprisingly, this plan developed significant surpluses. In the past they had been used to pay the company's contributions. The surpluses had arisen mainly because of the many years during which the plan's rate of return exceeded the actuarial assumption of 6 percent per year and because of the large profits realized when non-vested employees terminated their employment. The pension plan now has a very large surplus. Who owns it? Most people would say the employees.

In case two, the company has a non-contributory, final-average pension plan. Because of its concern to provide all benefits promised it has always funded the plan very strongly. Pensions in payment have been updated on a regular basis and the plan has always been kept up to date.

The plan has now developed a surplus because the historic actuarial assumptions have been so conservative. Revenue Canada has indicated that the company can make no further contributions until the surplus is reduced. Is the company justified in applying for a refund of surplus? It certainly seems more reasonable, doesn't it?

Many people argue that, once money has been deposited in a pension plan it is automatically the employees' money, held in trust for the day when it will be needed to provide pensions. If you agree with this point of view then you would have to say that refunds of surplus should never be allowed. Suppose that the provinces agreed with this, and banned all future refunds of surplus? How would employers react?

You will remember that when an actuary helps an employer decide on the rate of contribution to make to the pension plan, there is normally a considerable range of possible rates. This range extends from the minimum that the provincial authority will accept to the maximum Revenue Canada will permit as a tax deduction. Traditionally, most employers have not contributed at the minimum, reasoning that it is more important to have fairly level contributions from year to year than to pay the absolute minimum for a number of years and then have to make up the difference later. Employers took comfort in the knowledge that, if they really were overcontributing to the extent that the plan developed a large surplus, they could apply for (and normally expect to receive) a refund.

If the rules changed to disallow any future refunds, many employers would reduce their contribution rates. They would feel more comfortable in taking the risk of undercontributing to the plan.

Why have refunds become such a major issue? It is because of a strange set of circumstances that arose in the first half of the 1980s. Many companies suffered in the recession which caused widespread employee lay-offs. The financial effects of the recession were so bad in a number of industrial sectors that there was a real question whether some companies would be able to continue to operate. At the same time, rates of return were exceptionally high. This created a perfect situation for many pension funds. These funds made gains not only from the excess rates of return, but also from the termination of non-vested employees and because of the low salary increases granted to those who did stay employed. Hard-pressed employers suddenly saw a way to improve their finances. If they were making a loss anyway, they could apply for a refund of surplus and have it paid tax-free. Most of the provincial pension authorities were sympathetic, because they reasoned that it was better to refund a surplus than to insist it stay in the fund and then watch the company go out of business.

The trend continued throughout 1984 and 1985, with companies using various devices to increase the amount of the surplus available. The most common of these was to buy annuities for all the inactive employees, thus reducing the liability under the pension plan. In some cases the refunds were justifiable. In others, it really appeared that the employees were getting the short end of the stick. The only warning note was sounded by a number of trust companies who were concerned about the risk of class action suits at some future time when assets might not be sufficient to cover liabilities.

As frequently happens, the whole issue was brought to a head by one company that tried to push the rules to the limit. The Dominion Stores case of early 1986 gave such a high profile to the issue that it became clear steps had to be taken. The specific points at issue included:

- the wording of the trust agreement,
- the warning to be given to employees,
- the amount of the surplus attributable to the employees,
- the whole philosophical question of whether any surplus should ever be refundable.

The new legislation was being finalized in Ontario at about the same time. Not surprisingly it was strongly influenced by the need to settle the issue of refundable surplus.

In the first place, the Ontario legislation now requires that, before surplus can be refunded, the plan document must specifically permit the refund of surplus from an ongoing plan. Previously, it had been enough to show that the plan allowed for a surplus to revert to the employer when a plan was terminated. If an employer tried to amend the plan wording on this subject it must first send a copy of the proposed amendment to all employees who are plan members. Second, in Ontario the employer must advise employees in advance of an application for a refund and obtain an individual release from each employee. Third, in Ontario the employer can only apply for a refund of surplus over and above a minimum amount equal to the greater of two years' contributions or 25 percent of the liability for benefits earned to date. As well, the employer cannot apply for surplus that is attributable to the employees.

In December 1986 Ontario established the Friedland Task Force and banned refunds of surplus. Similar restrictions are in effect in most of the other provinces. In 1988 the Task Force recommended that approval for future refunds of surplus be an inducement for plan sponsors to provide retroactive indexing. This recommendation was incorporated in draft legislation, but has yet to be implemented.

What does the future hold? Will all future refunds be banned? At present, employers still have two strong arguments they can use. Pension plans are not mandatory. If an employer's pension plan has a large surplus and cannot obtain a refund, the plan can be wound-up.

Employers must fund "experience deficiencies" that arise when the experience is unfavourable. In the early 1970s, when most pension plans had negative rates of return, huge amounts were paid into pension funds. By the same token, employers argue, they should be entitled to a share of the profits in good times.

Why is this issue so important? Because we are talking about huge amounts which could be taken out of your pension fund.

Surpluses normally arise from high rates of return. To maintain goodwill, employers must make sure that, before they apply for future refunds, they have improved benefits to protect employees from the same economic forces that produced the rates of return. In other words, if the high rates of return arise from inflation, then the priority should be to protect the members.

A more recent issue has been the use of surplus to pay the required employer contributions; the so-called "contribution holiday". Despite the Revenue Canada ruling which prohibits employer contributions when a large surplus exists, many employees are questioning the employer's right to such a holiday.

20

Who Else Can Sponsor a Pension Plan?

*Idiots are always in favour of inequality of
income (their only chance for eminence) and the
really great in favour of equality.*

George Bernard Shaw

THROUGHOUT PART III WE HAVE CONCENTRATED on pension plans
sponsored by employers. This is still the most common type of private pension plan. However, there are others that are likely to gain
even more prominence in the future.

The opposite to the employer-sponsored plan is one that is
sponsored by a union. The plan is designed by the union and will
be available to all employees in that union. An employer who agrees
to participate has no control over how much he or she contributes.
This rate is established by the union's actuary, and is usually negotiated on a regular basis. These kinds of plans are called "multi-
employer" plans because many different employers will participate.

In the more common form of multi-employer plan there is a
joint board of trustees composed of representatives of both management and the union. All major decisions are made by this board,
including the appointment of the actuary, administrator, and investment manager. Frequently, both the benefit levels and the required
rates of contribution are set by negotiation.

There are a number of advantages to this type of plan. First, it
provides absolute portability of benefits for an employee moving
from one participating employer to another. Second, it provides
management and the union an opportunity to appreciate one anoth-

er's problems and to participate jointly in solving them. The joint board of trustees has to work at setting a funding strategy and an investment strategy that are aggressive and yet prudent. Administrative decisions are made in the knowledge of the implications of setting a precedent.

In a joint-trusteed plan like this, the member of the pension plan should never be surprised by a plan amendment that reduces any aspect of the benefits or by a refund of surplus. In theory, all decisions will have been agreed to in advance by the members' elected representatives.

What happens if one of the plan's participating employers goes out of business? Is there a risk that the employees could lose benefits because the employer's responsibility was limited to paying contributions at the required rate? No, in such a case the board of trustees takes the place of the employer in guaranteeing the benefits. The full financial resources of the plan would be available to meet the liability.

Many provinces have recommended increased employee involvement in the management of pension plans. There is speculation that this will mean more joint-trusteed plans involving one or more groups of employees.

If there is only one employee group involved, then we are looking at a hybrid plan. The trustees could not take overall responsibility for the security of benefits; this function would have to remain with the employer. However, in other respects there could be considerable advantages to setting up a joint-trusteed approach.

21

What if I Change Countries

*Travel, in the younger sort, is a part of
education; in the elder, a part of experience.*

Francis Bacon

UP TO THIS POINT WE HAVE ASSUMED that you will remain in
Canada for your working lifetime and will also retire here. Let's
consider what happens if you leave Canada or if you have moved
to Canada from another country. International benefit rules can
be complicated, so we will concentrate on what happens if you
move between Canada and the United States.

Private Pension Plans

If your employer asks you to relocate it is important to ask what
happens to your pension benefits. If you have worked in more than
one country there are generally two approaches used to make sure
that the whole period of service is covered.

First, the final plan in which you are a member may provide a
pension to cover your total period of service worldwide. The cost
of this pension will be reduced by any of the other pension payments you might receive from service in other plans.

Problems arise if the pension plans of your employer in various
countries are radically different. Suppose that the plan of the country you retire in is based on a 1.5 percent non-contributory final-
average formula, but that you had previously been in a 2 percent

contributory plan in another country. You might feel unfairly treated if your final pension is based on a formula for all service.

The second approach meets this problem. Under it you would be entitled to a pension payable from each country in which you had been employed, based on the years that you were in that country. There are also problems with this approach. Ideally you would like to retire with a total-service pension based on your earnings near retirement. Some companies may not be permitted by law, or may not want to base your pension on a salary over which they have no control, earned in another country.

Another issue is the risk of currency fluctuation. Your income in retirement could be very volatile if it is being paid in a number of different currencies. Try to have all pensions converted to the currency of the country in which you are living at the time you retire, for example, through the purchase of Canadian-dollar annuities.

Government Plans

Government benefits are simpler. In 1984 Canada concluded an agreement with the United States which rationalized the treatment of government plans for people who move between the two countries. The most recent, negotiated with Australia, is Canada's twenty-first agreement. Canada has concluded similar agreements with Austria, Barbados, Belgium, Denmark, Dominica, Finland, France, the Federal Republic of Germany, Greece, Iceland, Italy, Jamaica, Luxembourg, the Netherlands, Norway, Portugal, St. Lucia, Spain and Sweden. In the following sections we will analyze the Canada-United States treaty as it relates to contributions, OAS, CPP and U.S. Social Security.

Contributions

Before the agreement, if you were sent to the United States, you were required to contribute to U.S. Social Security even though you would probably never receive a benefit.

Now, if you expect to be in the United States for less than five years, you can choose to stay in the Canada/Quebec Pension Plan and be exempted from U.S. contributions. This can save you money and also help ensure that you receive a full Canada/Quebec Pension Plan benefit. Similar rules apply for someone relocated from the United States to Canada for less than five years.

Old Age Security

The rules governing Old Age Security were described in Part II. Under the rules, introduced on July 1, 1977, you receive an OAS pension equal to one-fortieth of the full pension multiplied by your number of years of Canadian residency after age eighteen to a maximum of forty years. To receive any benefit you must have been a resident in Canada for at least ten years after the age of eighteen. If you have been a resident of Canada for at least twenty years after age eighteen, you could have your pension paid to you anywhere in the world.

Before July 1, 1977, the rules granted you a full OAS pension, provided that you were a resident of Canada for the ten years immediately before retirement. If you were twenty-five or older on July 1, 1977, and lived in Canada before that date, you can choose to be covered by the old rules.

Under the agreement, years of participation under U.S. Social Security will not increase the amount of OAS benefit you receive; however, they can be used to establish your eligibility for benefits.

If you have lived in Canada for at least one year and have participated for at least ten years in U.S. Social Security and Canada/Quebec Pension Plan combined, you are eligible for an OAS benefit. The benefit would be one-fortieth of the full OAS pension multiplied by your years of Canadian participation.

If the combined period of Canadian and American coverage is at least twenty years, then the benefit can be paid to you indefinitely while you are living outside Canada.

The 1984 agreement does not apply to someone who opts to be covered by the old rules. For example, suppose you lived in the United States until you were age fifty-five and then moved to Canada before July 1, 1977, for your final ten working years. If you opt to be covered by the new rules, then you are eligible for a benefit of ten-fortieths (25 percent) of the full pension, payable anywhere in the world. If you opt to be covered by the old rules, you are eligible for a full OAS pension payable in Canada, but your pension would end if you moved back to the United States.

Canada/Quebec Pension Plan

Under the Canada/Quebec Pension Plan, there is no minimum required contribution period for a pension and the pension can be paid anywhere in the world. The 1984 agreement has very little impact on the Canada/Quebec Pension Plan. The only improvement is that periods of participation in U.S. Social Security can be used to establish eligibility for some of the non-pension benefits.

U.S. Social Security

To be eligible for U.S. Social Security benefits, you should have total participation of at least one calendar quarter times the number of years between 1951 and age sixty-two. For example, an individual aged sixty-three in 1984 would need thirty-two calendar quarters of participation (1983 − 1951 = 32).

The amount of the retirement pension is based on an individual's own Primary Insurance Amount determined from his or her Average Indexed Monthly Earnings in a similar way to the C/QPP calculation.

Under the 1984 agreement, periods of participation in the Canada/Quebec Pension Plan can now be used to establish eligibility for U.S. Social Security benefits, provided that you have contributed to the American program for at least six quarters. As before, the agreement does not have any effect on the amount of pension that would be paid.

As a result of the agreement, the United States will now pay benefits indefinitely in Canada to persons who are not citizens of the United States. The amount of the benefit paid by the United

States will be based on a formula that takes into account periods of contribution after 1936 to U.S. Social Security and periods of contribution to the Canada/Quebec Pension Plan.

In setting a strategy for your international pension, the key question is, "Where do you plan to live when you retire?" By planning ahead you can ensure that the majority of your private- and government-pension income will be paid in the appropriate currency and will, as far as possible, keep pace with the inflation of that country.

Calling All Britons

Unlike the rules governing U.S. citizens, British citizens who have moved to Canada and are eligible for a British pension have it frozen at the rate in effect when they first qualified. Only in Canada, you say? Not a bit of it. Britons who emigrated to Australia, New Zealand or South Africa receive similar treatment. In all, approximately 300,000 people are affected.

There is no logical explanation for this discrimination. Government representatives describe the situation as an "historical accident". Originally, in fact, all rights to a pension would be lost when an individual left Britain.

However, Benson Zonena, the President of the British Pensioners Association (Canada) is hopeful about a change. Under the new Representation of the People Act passed in 1989, British citizens living abroad can now vote in the next general election if their names were on an electoral register in the last 20 years. Their vote is in that constituency.

It is estimated that at least one million Britons have emigrated to Canada in the last 20 years. If you are eligible, what are you waiting for? Registration forms are available at the Consulate General offices in Toronto, Edmonton and Vancouver or the High Commission Office in Ottawa.

For more information call the British Pensioners Association (Canada) at (416) 253-6402.

The moral is, if you've lived in any other country for a significant length of time after age 18, it's worth checking to see if you have any additional pension entitlements.

22

How Good Is My Plan?

*An elegant sufficiency, content, retirement,
rural quiet, friendships.*

James Thomson

NOW THAT WE HAVE EXPLORED MOST ASPECTS of private pension plans, we are ready to tackle the big questions. Just how good is your company pension plan and, if it is optional, should you join?

Let's recap the key questions:

- What type of plan is it? Money-purchase, defined-benefit, multi-employer?
- How generous is the formula?
- Are employee contributions required?
- What is the normal retirement age?

The most generous defined-benefit plan permitted by Revenue Canada is one under which the benefit that will be paid is equal to your years of pensionable service times 2 percent times the average of your earnings in the best three consecutive years before you retire. The benefit can be paid from age sixty on an unreduced basis.

If you are offered this pension plan by your employer, and you don't have to contribute, then there is no doubt you should join.

Now for two fundamental questions:

1. If you are required to contribute a certain percentage of your pay to the pension plan, at what point does this stop being a good deal for you?

2. Would you be better off if you were not in the plan because then you could make the maximum contribution to a registered retirement savings plan?

Under any contributory, defined-benefit pension plan there will always be employees who think their contributions alone are paying for their pensions. Usually they are wrong. They have overlooked some aspect of the plan in their calculations.

Let's suppose you belong to a 2 percent final-average pension plan and that your required contribution is equal to 5 percent of pay. Suppose also that at retirement at age sixty-five, $1 of pension income will be worth $10.

If you join the pension plan at age thirty with a salary of $20,000, let's estimate that you will receive annual salary increases of 5 percent and that you will obtain a rate of return of 6 percent on your contributions. Your pension at age sixty-five will be equal to 35 years × 2 percent × $95,000 (your final-average salary) or $66,500 per year. This will be worth $665,000.

What will your personal contributions with interest be worth? This is a complicated calculation. The first contribution will be 5 percent of $20,000 or $1,000. This will earn interest at 6 percent for thirty-five years and will be worth $7,686. The second contribution will be 5 percent of $21,000 or $1,050. This will earn interest at 6 percent for thirty-four years and will be worth $7,614.

If we accumulate all of your contributions we will have a total value of $230,000, approximately one-third the value of the pension. If salary increases had been at 6 percent, then the value of the pension at retirement would increase to $904,000 and the value of the contribution would only increase to $269,000, approximately 30 percent of the value of the pension.

This example illustrates the sensitivity of the calculation to the assumptions made. Often an employee forgets to allow for future salary increases and assumes a very high long-term rate of return, say 10 percent. Under those assumptions the position would be quite different. The pension would be $20,000 × 2 percent × 35 years or $14,000 with a value of $140,000. Your contributions would have a value of $298,000. You would be buying your pension twice over.

Apart from the difficulties of deciding on the assumptions to use, the typical case is much more complex than the example given. The plan might be integrated with the Canada Pension Plan, so might your contributions. The plan might be career-averaged. Should you allow for future upgrades in benefits? Probably yes, if they have been made in the past.

A very rough rule of thumb — the "nine times" rule — is provided in the tax rules effective January 1, 1991. As we have said, this rule holds that, on average, taken over all active pension plan members, $1 of pension earned is equivalent to a contribution of $9. This rule is based on the unlikely assumption that the pension will be indexed to the cost of living after retirement.

For your purposes we suggest the "six times" rule. Calculate the pension you will earn in the coming year based on your present salary and multiply the answer by six. Compare the result to the amount of contribution you will be asked to make.

In our example an individual aged thirty would do the following calculation:

Amount of pension to be earned in the coming year =
2 percent × $20,000 = $400.
Value now: 6 × 400 = $2,400.
Contribution required: $1,000.

Conclusion? This employee is paying for less than half of the pension. The plan is a good deal!

Your decision about whether or not to join your employer's pension plan will also be affected by your feelings about your employer. If you don't plan to stay more than a year, don't join. If you plan to stay more than two years then joining the plan could make sense. You are guaranteed the value of your contributions, and the employer will fund half of the pension you have earned. But be careful. Your contributions could be "locked in" until you retire. Keep this in mind.

As a final rule of thumb, remember that a defined-benefit plan gives better value to an older employee than a younger employee. If you join a company later in your career and you have the chance to join a defined-benefit plan it will usually be to your advantage.

Tax Implications

So far we have looked at the value you would receive from joining a pension plan. But there is another angle.

Under the new tax rules, an individual who belongs to a defined-benefit pension plan will have his or her maximum RRSP contribution reduced by the value of the pension accrued in the previous year, called the pension adjustment. Many salaried pension plan members, particularly commissioned salespeople, reacted by saying they want to opt out of their pension plans. The reason isn't value, but rather lost opportunity.

Does this argument makes any sense? Consider the case of John, a forty-year-old member of a non-contributory 1 percent final-average pension plan earning $50,000 a year. Let's look at John's options. Once again we'll assume an annual salary increase of 5 percent in the future, that contributions can earn 6 percent, and that the $15,500 contribution maximum will be indexed in the future.

The pension John can earn for future service in the pension plan is 25 × 1 percent × final-average salary ($146,200) or $36,550 with a value of, say, $365,500. His pension adjustment will be 9 percent of pay less $1,000. If he also contributes the maximum possible amount per year to an RRSP, the accumulated value will be $490,000, for a total value at retirement of $855,500 ($365,500 + $490,000).

Now, suppose instead, John opts out of the pension plan and contributes 18 percent of his annual earnings to an RRSP. The value at retirement will be $864,000.

So how does this option stack up? If John stays in the plan, he will be slightly worse off, but will have made a reduced contribution.

Money-Purchase Plans

The decision whether or not to join a defined-contribution or money-purchase plan is usually far easier to make. Frequently employee contributions are matched by employer contributions according to some formula. The employee can see a clear advantage to joining such a plan. The only risk is that contributions will be locked in after termination. If the employee contributed instead to an RRSP he or she could remove contributions at will, but, of course, would receive no company contributions.

The other risk inherent in joining an employer-sponsored defined-contribution plan is that you will be required to invest your assets in a choice of one or more vehicles established by your employer. Although these vehicles will normally have been chosen with a good deal of care, there is no guarantee that they will outperform those selected by your personal investment manager.

PART IV

PERSONAL SAVINGS

23

How Much Should I Save?

There is a tide in the affairs of men, which,
taken at the flood, leads on to fortune.

Shakespeare

NOW WE COME TO THE SECTION OF THE BOOK in which you, the
reader, should do some work. You have to ask yourself, "Is the
income I will receive in retirement going to be enough to support
my planned lifestyle?" With the information you have gained in
this book you should be able to arrive at an answer.

If you decide there is a shortfall you will have to decide how to
make up the difference:

- by participating in a savings plan or a second-tier pension
  plan provided by your employer;
- by contributing to a Registered Retirement Savings Plan.

You will also need to decide how much you are going to save on a
regular basis to meet your goal. Savings patterns vary by individual, but we will assume that you will set up a program that will
require an annual contribution equal to a level percentage of your
pay between now and retirement.

You can use a four-step approach to see how well you are doing.

Step 1 — Decide how much *after-tax* (net) income you will need
when you retire.

Step 2 — Calculate how much *after-tax* (net) income you will receive when you retire. Include income from government pension programs, employer programs, and from any other sources.

Step 3 — Calculate the amount of *pre-tax* (gross) income you will need in retirement to make up the difference between 1) and 2).

Step 4 — Establish a program that will allow you to build up the amount required for 3).

Step 1

Many books have been written about the need for pre-retirement planning. Now is your chance to imagine yourself in retirement. Will your house be paid off? Will you be renting an apartment? Will your lifestyle be the same as it is now? Will you be touring the world in a minibus? Will you be working at a part-time job or will you be living a life of leisure?

Put your imagination to work. Dream of yourself in retirement at this moment. Just how much income would you need to support yourself after all taxes are paid? Your answer may be different depending on whether you plan to retire at age sixty-five or earlier. This will also affect the level of income you will receive.

Let's suppose that Harry March is doing this exercise. You will remember that he was born in 1947 and that he is currently earning $44,000 per year.

Harry and Alice plan to retire in twenty-one years when Harry is sixty-five. Like many of us, they do not have a clear picture of their retirement. They like the idea of spending part of each year in Florida and summers with their grandchildren. Logic tells them that their costs will not be as high as when they are working. They will not need so many dress clothes, their commuting fares will be a thing of the past and their mortgage will be paid off. They agree that, as a guess, they will need 80 percent of their joint take-home pay just before they retire.

Assuming future salary increases at a rate of 5 percent per year, Harry's final salary will be about $123,000. He currently has total deductions from his gross pay equal to $12,000, which includes income tax, Canada Pension Plan contributions, Unemployment Insurance contributions, and contributions to his company pension plan of $2,200 in 1991. He estimates that, when he is sixty-four, his total deductions from pay will be $43,000, giving him a net take-home pay of $80,000. His target after-tax retirement income is $64,000 (80 percent of $80,000).

Step 2

In Step 2, Harry calculates his expected income in retirement from:

- the Canada Pension Plan;
- Old Age Security;
- the company pension plan.

You may remember that Harry will be eligible for the full Canada Pension Plan and Old Age Security pension. He estimates that these will be equal to $20,000 and $12,000 respectively when he is sixty-five. In Part III we showed that Harry's company pension earned to date is $9,000. He estimates that his pension for future service will be $29,500. His total expected pension income is:

Canada Pension	$20,000	
Old Age Security	$12,000	
Company Pension	$38,500	($29,500 + $9,000)
Total Expected Pension	$70,500	

Harry guesses that the tax he will pay as a retired individual based on this total pension income is $14,500, giving him an expected net income in retirement of $56,000. The difference between his desired net income ($64,000) and his expected net pension income ($56,000) is $8,000. This is the amount that will have to be made up by Harry's additional savings.

Step 3

Harry decides that he will make up this difference by contributions to an RRSP. The advantages of this type of plan over a regular savings account are that his contributions should be tax deductible and the investment income should be tax exempt. However, the ultimate income will be taxable. Harry estimates that he will need to provide a gross, pre-tax income of $10,000 in order to enjoy his additional $8,000 after tax.

Step 4

In this final step Harry has to decide what percentage of pay to save over twenty-one years in order to provide a gross income of $10,000. He decides to assume that his contributions will earn interest at 7 percent per year and that, at retirement, $1 of pension income will cost him $10.

On this basis, Harry calculates tha a future contribution of 1 percent of pay will buy him an additional pension of $3,300 per year. He now knows that, based upon the various assumptions he has made, an additional contribution of 3 percent of pay will be enough for him to meet his retirement objective (3 × $3,300 = $9,900).

Because Harry is a prudent man, he will probably check these calculations every few years to make sure he is on track. As he gets older he and Alice will also firm up their retirement plans and he may want to adjust his original 80 percent target.

One important point here is that Harry has ignored the possibility of his employer making future updates to the career-average formula. If, in fact, his pension is updated to some type of final-average basis close to retirement then, because of his anticipated thirty-nine years of service with the insurance company, he would probably not need any additional savings to reach his target level of retirement income.

Now It's Your Turn

As you read the last section and saw Harry making assumptions about the future with such confidence, you might have wondered if he was taking actuarial exams by correspondence course! The chief difficulty was projecting all of his calculations twenty-one years into the future and estimating the future levels of salary increases, interest rates, government pension benefits, and tax rates.

For your purposes we suggest a short cut. As you do the calculations, pretend that it is the day before you retire, that you are earning your present salary and that current tax rates and government benefit levels apply. By working in today's dollars you will find the calculations much easier. Let's go back and see how you might tackle each step.

Step 1 — How Much Will I Need?

Step 1 really is up to you. If you are a long way from retirement it may be sufficient to assume, just as Harry did, that you will need 80 percent of your current net take-home pay to meet your needs in retirement. If you are over fifty then you may well have a very clear plan for your retirement. Go through the exercise in some detail. It will show you whether your plans are financially viable, or if you have some rethinking to do.

Step 2 — How Much Will I Receive?

Under the provincial consensus employers are required to provide annual pension statements to plan members. If you are a member of a defined-benefit pension plan this will give you exactly what you need. You can use your projected company pension based on current earnings and the estimates of your Canada/Quebec Pension Plan and Old Age Security benefits to give you your total projected pension based on current earnings.

If you are a member of a defined-benefit plan and for some reason, you have not received a pension statement, then you can always produce the numbers for yourself. Suppose you are a member of a 1 percent final-average pension plan. Remember that you are projecting your pension at retirement based on your *current* earnings. If you will have twenty-five years of credited service from joining the plan to retirement, then your projected pension is 25 percent of your current pay. In order to project the Canada/Quebec Pension Plan and Old Age Security benefits you should use the current values of these pensions. You can also use these amounts to make allowance for any integration in your basic pension formula. When you go through this exercise, you should remember the value of any paid-up pensions you have earned from previous pension plans.

Finally, if your plans call for you to retire before age sixty-five, remember to make allowance for the effect this will have on all your pensions. Your pension plan booklet will tell you if your basic pension will be reduced because of your early retirement. Sometimes you can still receive an unreduced pension if you have sufficient years of service; it will depend on your particular plan design. The Canada/Quebec Pension Plan can also be taken early, but with a reduction of 0.5 percent per month between the ages of sixty and sixty-five. The Old Age Security benefit cannot be taken until age sixty-five. Similar remarks apply if you plan to retire after age sixty-five, except that the reductions will become increases.

If your basic pension plan is a defined-contribution plan or a hybrid arrangement, then your pension statement will give you little idea of the ultimate pension you can expect from your pension plan. It will, however, show you your current balance in the plan. To try to project this pension to retirement as simply as possible, we will assume that the rate of return you will receive on your money will be equal to your rate of salary increase.

To project the annual pension from your current plan balance, simply divide the balance by ten. For example, if you have a balance of $20,000 this will convert into a pension of $2,000. To project the pension from your future contributions, take the total contribution you and your employer will make in the current calendar year on your behalf. Multiply by the number of years to retirement and divide by 10. For example, if your joint contribution for 1987 is $4,000 and you have twenty years to retirement, then your projected pension is $4,000 × 20 ÷ 10, or $8,000. This will give you a total projected pension of $10,000 ($2,000 plus $8,000).

Once again, retirement before or after age sixty-five will affect the level of your pension. The factor of 10 is suitable if you plan to retire at age sixty-five. Alternative factors based on your expected age at retirement are:

Retirement Age	Pension Factor
55	12
60	11
65	10
70	9

Your income will be lower when you retire. But you will also be entitled to more deductions in retirement and you will not be required to make contributions to many of the government programs. Your income taxes will be lower when you retire than they are when you are working.

At the end of step 2 you will have a clear picture of your expected after-tax pension income in retirement.

Step 3—What Is the Difference Between What I Need and What I Will Receive?

You will remember that, in this step, you compare the after-tax income you need with the after-tax income you anticipate. Then figure out how much additional gross income you need to generate from various sources, to make up the shortfall.

As you look at your own position it may well be that your requirements in retirement fluctuate as a result of, say, paying off your mortgage at a certain age. Similarly, your anticipated income may change during retirement as you become eligible to receive different government or private pension-plan benefits. In most cases we would expect that you could calculate a shortfall prior to age sixty-five and a different shortfall after age sixty-five, since many of the expected changes will occur at that age.

The process of moving from a net shortfall to a gross shortfall can be made as simple or as sophisticated as you wish. At the simple level you can use a ratio like 80 percent the way Harry did. Remember how he converted a net shortfall of $8,000 to a gross shortfall of $10,000? After all, it may be many years until you retire. At the sophisticated level, you can try a process of trial and error with the tax tables until you calculate the required level of additional gross income. If necessary, you can perform the calculation separately for the pre-sixty-five and post-sixty-five situations, since the change in certain tax deductions and contributions to government programs may change your marginal tax rate.

Step 4—How Shall I Make Up This Difference?

If you are still persevering with these calculations, the end is in sight! Once you know your required additional gross income, you multiply by the pension factor and divide by the number of years to retirement to obtain your annual savings requirement. The pension factors are as shown under Step 2, ranging from twelve at age fifty-five to nine at age seventy.

Suppose you are now aged forty-five and you wish to retire at fifty-five, and you calculate that you need $4,000 per year from age fifty-five to sixty-five and $2,000 per year from age sixty-five onwards. You would treat this as a pension of (i) $4,000 payable from age fifty-five less a pension of (ii) $2,000 payable from age sixty-five.

This will require annual contributions of:

(i) $4,000 × 12 ÷ 10 or $4,800
less
(ii) $2,000 × 10 ÷ 10 or $2,000
for a total of $2,800 each year up to age fifty-five.

If you are earning $35,000 you must contribute 8 percent of pay for the next ten years.

As a final point, we must remind you that all our calculations have assumed that you will be able to obtain a tax-free build-up on your additional contributions and that the resulting income will be taxable. This approach is ideally suited for a situation in which you have the tax "room" available to make your contributions through an RRSP. In other situations you may have to use your ingenuity to make the necessary adjustments.

Like any aspect of pension funding, you should not complete this procedure once and then follow it doggedly for twenty years. The whole process should be repeated at least once every three years to ensure that your savings program is on track. Your needs may change, your pension plan may change, your job may change.

24

Riffling Through the RRIFs

Taxes are what we pay for a civilized society.
Oliver Wendell Holmes

REGISTERED RETIREMENT INCOME FUNDS or RRIFs were introduced in 1978 in response to a demand for a tax-deferred investment channel which offered some investment flexibility for money from a maturing Registered Retirement Savings Plan.

At that time, the only options available were either to take the money as cash, pay tax on it, or use it to buy a life annuity from an insurance company and pay tax on the monthly income. The new RRIF was not dependent on life contingencies and could be issued by banks and trust companies as well as insurance companies.

The original concept behind a RRIF was to spread gradually increasing payments over the years between the time the RRIF was established and age 90. This was achieved by following a fixed formula used to calculate the amount of withdrawal each year.

For example, if you set up a $100,000 RRIF at age 70 (and so have 20 years to reach 90), your withdrawal in the first year must be $5,000 ($100,000/20). The payout in the second year would be the value of the fund, with interest, divided by 19, and so on. Thus, there will be nothing left in the RRIF by the time you reach age 90.

Investment income within the plan is tax-sheltered, so the rate of return is calculated on the total amount. Assuming the annual rate of return exceeds the rate of inflation, the RRIF is similar to an indexed annuity for a certain term.

Unfortunately, the RRIF did not prove to be a success. Consumers found the level of payouts in the early years to be lower than life annuity payments, which also had the advantage of being payable indefinitely. Over the next few years a number of attempts were made to modify the RRIF, but the results only served to complicate the product rather than to make it more popular.

In February, 1986, the federal budget introduced several changes which substantially improved the RRIF's flexibility. Two in particular contributed directly to the rapid rise in the RRIF's popularity. First, the mandatory payout was converted to a minimum for any particular year, effectively allowing the holder to take out as much as needed. Second, individuals were permitted to have as many RRIFs as they wished, allowing them to diversify among institutions as well as investments. It also allowed for self-directed RRIFs. These changes open up the possibility of structuring levels of retirement income which meet almost any financial plan.

For example, suppose an individual took out a RRIF in 1969 at age 71. The plan would then have matured in 1988, when the holder reached age 90. Table 1 shows the level of payments each year under the plan, starting with an initial deposit of $100,000, assuming the RRIF was invested 50% in the equities underlying the TSE 300 Index, 40% in mid-term bonds, and 10% in Treasury bills. (This is not necessarily a suitable investment mix for everyone; it is for illustration only).

Clearly, the payouts increased at a faster rate than inflation over the twenty year period. Not surprisingly, analysis demonstrates that investment in equities would have given the highest level of payouts over the period, closely followed by investment in T-bills, with bonds lagging a long way behind. However, it would be an aggressive investor, especially at that age, who would want to commit 100% of his future retirement income to equities.

Whatever you choose to invest in, there is a critical issue to contend with: what to do in the event that you reach age 90 and payouts suddenly cease. The problem is more difficult because the decisions cannot be left until you approach that age. You must prepare for the event when you set up your RRIF.

One option is to base the minimum withdrawals from the RRIF on your spouse's age (if lower) instead of your own. For example, if your spouse is age 60 when you are 70, the RRIF would last for 30 years, not 20.

There are other options. You may decide to use part of the money from your maturing RRSP to buy a life annuity. It offers a dual advantage: first, it allows the individual to keep as much money as possible in the tax-protected RRIF by reducing withdrawals to a minimum; and second, it continues at least a minimum level of income if the holder lives beyond age 90.

Another alternative is to take the money out of the RRIF and buy a stripped bond or other security which matures at age 90. It would then provide a lump sum at age 90, with which the holder could buy a life annuity.

We would have thought that a potential solution would be to buy a deferred annuity payable at age 90 — the price should certainly be right! However, our research has shown that there are no insurance companies currently offering this product.

Perhaps this issue isn't as critical as it may appear. Many people who have bought RRIFs since the legislation was changed have apparently taken payouts at a much faster rate than the minimum levels. Maybe they have other arrangements for their later retirement years.

In any event, just as the character of the RRIF has changed in the last few years, it is highly likely that more changes will occur in the future. For instance, consider the impact of pension reform. Shorter minimum vesting periods mean more employees will leave service with entitlement to a deferred vested pension. Portability rules give them the right to transfer these amounts into locked-in RRSPs.

Currently, locked-in RRSPs cannot be converted to a RRIF, but must be used to buy a life annuity. However, there's nothing to stop a provincial government from introducing RRIFs as an option. Could this lead to the introduction of a "locked-in RRIF", featuring the original compulsory payment rules to prevent the total amount being paid out prematurely?

RRIFs could also become an alternative to indexed annuities as a means of indexing money purchase and deferred profit sharing plans. Many options seem possible in the post-reform environment in which we are operating.

Regardless of the actual course of future provincial and federal legislation, it is clear that RRIFs are becoming an increasingly popular and more lucrative alternative to life annuities. A recent survey of banks and trust companies showed that most of them are currently planning to update their RRIF products and are preparing glossy brochures to sell them to a waiting world.

TABLE 1
RRIF ILLUSTRATION

Year	Opening Balance	Investment Income	Annual Payout	Closing Balance
	$'000	$'000	$'000	$'000
1969	100.00	.34	− 5.00	95.34
1970	95.34	7.32	− 5.02	97.64
1971	97.64	8.82	− 5.42	101.04
1972	101.04	14.60	− 5.94	109.70
1973	109.70	1.10	− 6.86	103.94
1974	103.94	− 13.75	− 6.93	83.26
1975	83.26	9.77	− 5.95	87.08
1976	87.08	12.21	− 6.70	92.59
1977	92.59	7.53	− 7.72	92.40
1978	92.40	14.79	− 8.40	98.79
1979	98.79	22.09	− 9.88	111.00
1980	111.00	19.05	− 12.33	117.72
1981	117.72	− 5.12	− 14.72	97.88
1982	97.88	21.05	− 13.98	104.95
1983	104.95	23.70	− 17.49	111.16
1984	111.16	7.53	− 22.23	96.46
1985	96.46	23.36	− 24.11	95.71
1986	95.71	11.34	− 31.90	75.15
1987	75.15	3.39	− 37.57	40.97
1988	40.97	4.17	− 45.14	−

Conclusion

*My interest is in the future because I am going to
spend the rest of my life there.*

Charles F. Kettering

AFTER READING THIS BOOK you should have obtained a broad overview of the Canadian pension system. You have seen how the total
public and private system has evolved as a compromise between:

- the needs of employees following the breakdown of the
  extended family;
- the needs of employers to formalize retirement arrangements
  and to obtain favourable tax treatment;
- the needs of government to respond to the concerns of voters.

The first milestone was reached in the mid-1960s with the introduction of pension legislation by a number of the provinces and
the creation of the Canada/Quebec Pension Plan. These developments lasted for twenty years with few significant changes.

Over the twenty years, however, the need for change in the system was growing:

- inflation became a major issue;
- the female proportion of the workforce increased dramatically;
- the workforce became more mobile;
- life-expectancy improved;
- society as a whole demanded more flexibility.

The end product of many years of debate has arrived. The provincial acts were updated to meet these pressures. The Canada Pension Plan was overhauled and the whole tax system governing pension plans has been revised. The politicians that we spoke to believe that these changes are fundamental enough to create another twenty-year dynasty.

Why is this important to you? Three reasons! First, because many of the rules have changed, now is an ideal time to learn how the pension system works. What you learn now should be relevant for the next twenty years. Second, because the new system has built in such fundamental changes, it will require the revision, if not the complete redesign of every pension plan in Canada. Since this will affect your pension, you should be able to understand the material your employer gives you. Third, in this era of increased flexibility you will be faced with many more options. The decisions you make will have a profound influence on your final pension. We hope that, as a result of reading this book, the decisions you make will be right for your situation.

If you have questions that this book does not address, contact us. It will help us in the future.

We wish you the retirement you want!

Appendix I

Pension Legislation by Province for Company-Sponsored Defined-Benefit Plans

	Federal	Alberta	Ontario	Quebec	Manitoba	Saskatchewan	Nova Scotia & Newfoundland
Eligibility for Membership	After 24 months with earnings at least 35% of YMPE (incl. part-time)	After 2 consecutive calendar years with earnings at least 35% of YMPE (incl. part-time)	After 24 months with earnings at least 35% of YMPE (incl. part-time)	After one calendar year with earnings at least 35% of YMPE (incl. part-time)	Compulsory after 2 consecutive calendar years with earnings at least 25% of YMPE (incl. part-time)	No rule	No rule
Minimum Interest on Contributions	Minimum rate of interest on employee contributions (as prescribed)	Minimum rate of interest on employee contributions (as prescribed)	Minimum rate of interest on employee contributions (as prescribed)	Minimum rate of interest on employee contributions (as prescribed)	Minimum rate of interest on employee contributions (as prescribed)	Minimum rate of interest on employee contributions (as prescribed)	No rule
Minimum Employer Cost	Employer must pay 50% of value of pension credits unless inflation protection of 75% of CPI above 1% is promised	Employer must pay 50% of value of pension credits	Employer must pay 50% of value of pension credits	Employer must pay 50% of value of pension credits	Employer must pay 50% of value of pension credits	Employer must pay 50% of value of pension credits	No rule
Disposition of Excess on Termination	Increase pension or transfer	Refund, transfer or (if plan provides) increase pension	Refund	Increase pension or transfer	Refund, increase pension or transfer	Transfer, purchase an annuity or increase pension	
Vesting	2 years membership	5 years service	2 years membership	2 years membership	2 years service	Age + service = 45 with 1 year service	45 + 10
Portability	Portability of vested benefits	Portability of vested benefits	Portability of vested benefits	Portability of vested benefits	Portability of vested benefits	No rule	No rule

Survivor Benefits After Retirement	May reduce to 60% of accrued benefit on first death; actuarial adjustment permitted	May reduce to 60% of accrued benefit on first death; actuarial adjustments permitted	May reduce to 60% on first death; actuarial adjustments permitted	May reduce to 60% of accrued benefit on death of member: actuarial adjustments permitted	May reduce to 66⅔% of accrued benefit on first death: actuarial adjustments permitted	May reduce to 50% of accrued benefit on death of member: actuarial adjustments permitted	No rule
Death Benefits Before Retirement	Commuted value of amount employee entitled to had he left service at death (incl. value of benefit arising from 50% rule) is payable to surviving spouse	60% of the commuted value of vested pension to provide a pension to surviving spouse; otherwise, lump sum to beneficiary or estate	Commuted value of vested benefits to spouse; otherwise to estate	Commuted value of vested benefits (incl. value of benefit arising from 50% rule) to named beneficiary or estate	Commuted value of vested benefits to surviving spouse to provide a life annuity; otherwise, payment to beneficiary or estate	No rule	No rule
Normal Retirement	Specific age at which pension received without reduction	Specific age at which pension received without reduction	Not later than 6 months after 65th birthday	No later than 1st day of the month after age 65	Specific age	No rule	No rule
Early Retirement	Within 10 years normal retirement	Within 5 years of normal retirement	Within 10 years of normal retirement	Within 10 years of normal retirement	Subject to reasonable age and service requirements	No rule	No rule
Postponed Retirement	Service and salary must be taken into account in calculating pension	Actuarial adjustment of pension plus further accruals	Member may continue membership and continue to accrue pension benefits according to plan formula	Pension revalorized: if contributions paid during postponement, additional pension purchased with contributions: all or part of pension can commence during postponement	Continue contributions to enhance pension	No rule	No rule

Appendix II
Provincial Pension Commissions

Alberta   Ms. Lesley Bowering
                        Acting Superintendent of Pensions
                        Alberta Labour
                        Employment/Pensions Branch
                        Room 401
                        10808-99 Avenue
                        Edmonton, alberta
                        T4K 0G5
                        403-427-8322

British Columbia   Mr. John Cook
                        Commissioner of Pensions
                        Superannuation Commission
                        544 Michigan Street
                        Victoria, B.C.
                        V8V 4R4
                        604-387-1002

Manitoba   Mr. John Cumberford
                        Superintendent of Pensions
                        Pension Commission of Manitoba
                        Room 1004
                        401 York Avenue.
                        Winnipeg, Manitoba
                        R3C 0P8
                        204-945-2740

New Brunswick	Ms. Danielle Merivier
	Registrar of Pensions
	N.B. Department of Labour
	P.O. Box 6000
	470 York St.
	Fredericton, N.B.
	E3B 5H1
	506-453-2055

Nova Scotia

Mr. Percy Fleet
Superintendent of Pensions
Government of the Province of Nova Scotia
P.O. Box 187
Halifax, Nova Scotia
B3J 2N3
902-424-5704

Ontario

Mr. Robert Hawkes
Superintendent of Pensions
Pension Commission of Ontario
101 Bloor Street West
9th Floor
Toronto, Ontario
M7A 2K2
416-963-0522

Quebec

M. Claude Legault
President, Quebec Pension Board
P.O. Box 5200
Quebec, Quebec
G1K 7S9
418-643-8302

Saskatchewan

Mr. Art Milne
Acting Superintendent of Pensions
Human Resources, Labour and Employment
1870 Albert Street
Regina, Saskatchewan
S4P 3V7
306-787-2458

References

Cooper, Keith H., and Colin C. Mills, *Canada at the Pension Crossroads* (New York: Financial Executives Research Foundation, 1978).

Financial Executives Institute, *Private Pension Plans and the Public Interest* (New York, 1967).

Freeman, Richard B., and James Medoff, *What Do Unions Do?* (New York: Basic Books, 1984).

Frith, Douglas, C., Notes for a speech to the International Foundation of Employee Benefit Plans, Ottawa, May 5, 1986.

Green, Fiona Lamont, *A Teacher's Resource Guide on Aging* (Toronto: Help the Aged, 1982).

Hamilton, Colleen, and John Whalley, "Reforming Public Pensions in Canada: Issues and Options" in *Pensions Today and Tomorrow: Background Studies*, edited by D.W. Conklin, J.H. Bennett, and T.J. Courchene (Toronto: Ontario Economic Council, 1984).

Health and Welfare Canada/Department of Finance, *Better Pensions for Canadians* (Ottawa: Supply and Services, 1982).

Health and Welfare Canada/Department of Finance, *The Canada Pension Plan: Keeping It Financially Healthy* (Ottawa: Supply and Services Canada, 1985).

Healy, C. Ross, "Pensions and the Capital Markets: Independence or Intervention?" in *Pensions Today and Tomorrow: Background*

Studies, edited by D.W. Conklin, J.H. Bennett, and T.J. Courchene (Toronto: Ontario Economic Council, 1984).

Hellyer, Paul, excerpts from a forthcoming autobiography.

Kehoe, Frank, and Maurice Archer, *Canadian Industrial Relations* (Oakville: Twentieth Century Labour Publications, 1983).

LaMarsh, Judy, *Memoirs of a Bird in a Gilded Cage* (Toronto: McClelland and Stewart, 1969).

National Council of Welfare on the Incomes of the Aged, *Sixty-Five and Older* (Ottawa: Supply and Services, 1984).

Nixon, Robert, "Canada Pension Plan Reform," extracts from a speech by the Treasurer of Ontario to the Canadian Pension Conference, January 17, 1986.

Statistics Canada, *Pension Plans in Canada 1988*, Cat no. 74-401 (Ottawa: Supply and Services, 1990).

Task Force on Pension Reform, *Report* (Ottawa: Supply and Services, 1982).

Task Force on Retirement Income Policy, *The Retirement Income in Canada: Problems and Alternative Policies for Reform* (Ottawa: Supply and Services, 1980).

Treasurer of Ontario, *Canada Pension Plan: Statutory Actuarial Report No. 8*, as at December 31, 1982, tabled in the House of Commons, June 5, 1984.

Treasurer of Ontario, *Ontario Proposals for Pension Reform* (Toronto: Queen's Printer, 1980).

Wyatt et al., *Employee Retirement Plans* (Washington: Graphic Arts Press, 1945).

Index

Printed in Canada